Taste of Home

COOKING SCHOOL

COOKBOOK

TASTE OF HOME BOOKS • RDA ENTHUSIAST BRANDS, LLC • MILWAUKEE, WI

International Standard Book Number:
978-1-62145-889-0

Chief Content Officer, Home & Garden:
Jeanne Sidner
Content Director: Mark Hagen
Associate Creative Director: Raeann Thompson
Senior Editor: Christine Rukavena
Editors: Amy Glander, Hazel Wheaton
Senior Art Director: Courtney Lovetere
Designer: Carrie Peterson
Deputy Editor, Copy Desk: Dulcie Shoener
Senior Copy Editor: Ann Walter

Photographer: Dan Roberts
Set Stylist: Melissa Franco
Food Stylist: Sarah Fischer

Pictured on back cover:
Classic Avocado Toast, p. 238; Frozen Margaritas,
p. 22; Seasoned Roast Turkey, p. 125; Cheesy
Broccoli Soup in a Bread Bowl, p. 54; Garlic
Mashed Red Potatoes, p. 213

Printed in China
1 3 5 7 9 10 8 6 4 2

CONTENTS

BASIC KNIFE SKILLS

Discover the essential knives for your collection, and learn about knife care and handling, plus key cutting techniques

▲ **Mincing** Pieces no larger than ⅛ in.

COMMON CUTTING & CHOPPING TECHNIQUES

MINCING AND CHOPPING

- Holding the chef's knife with a power grip (see p. 5), rest the fingers of your other hand on the top of the blade near the tip.
- Using the handle to guide and apply pressure, move knife in an arc across the food with a rocking motion until food is chopped to the desired size.

DICING AND CUBING VEGETABLES

- Using a chef's knife, trim each side of the vegetable, squaring it off. Cut lengthwise into evenly spaced strips. The narrower the strips, the smaller the pieces will be.
- Stack the strips and cut lengthwise into uniformly sized strips.
- Arrange the square-shaped strips into a pile and cut widthwise into uniform cubes.

MAKING BIAS OR DIAGONAL CUTS

- Holding a chef's or paring knife at an angle to the food, slice as thick or thin as desired, using a control grip (see p. 5). This technique is often used in stir-fry recipes.

MAKING JULIENNE STRIPS

- Using a chef's knife, cut a thin strip from 1 side of vegetable. Turn so the vegetable sits flat.
- Cut vegetable into thin, even slices of the desired length (usually 2 in.).
- Stack the slices and cut lengthwise into thin strips.

CUTTING WEDGES

- Using a chef's knife or serrated knife, cut the produce in half from stem end to the blossom end. Lay halves cut side down on a cutting board. Cut each half vertically into thirds.

ZESTING

- Pull a citrus zester across limes, lemons or oranges, being careful not to remove the bitter white pith. Chop strips into fine pieces if desired. Or use the finest side of a box grater.

◄ **Chopping** ¼- to ½-in. pieces

▶ **Bias/ Diagonal Cuts** Size of pieces based on desired length and thickness

◄ **Cubing** ½- to 1-in. uniform pieces

▼ **Dicing** ⅛- to ¼-in. uniform pieces

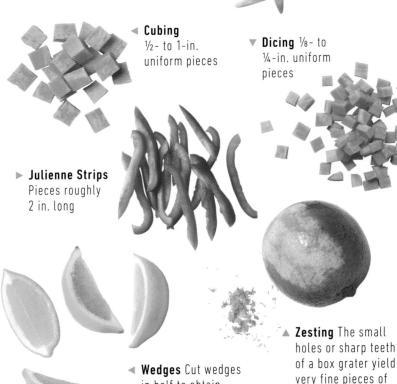

▶ **Julienne Strips** Pieces roughly 2 in. long

◄ **Wedges** Cut wedges in half to obtain desired thickness

▲ **Zesting** The small holes or sharp teeth of a box grater yield very fine pieces of citrus zest

ESSENTIAL CUTLERY

Good knives are a must for any well-equipped kitchen. Here are the basics for building your collection.

▲ **Steel:** This long, thin rod with a handle is used to smooth out small rough spots on the edge of a knife blade and to reset the edge. After the steel, you might add a whetstone or electric sharpener to hone your knives.

▼ **Chef's Knife:** This 8-in. to 10-in. multipurpose knife is used for chopping, dicing and mincing.

▼ **Paring Knife:** This 3- to 4-in. knife is used for peeling, mincing and slicing small foods.

▲ **Serrated or Bread Knife:** This knife's serrated blade is used for slicing breads, cakes and delicate foods like tomatoes. An 8-in. blade is most versatile, but a range of lengths are available.

▼ **Kitchen Shears** This versatile tool is used to snip fresh herbs, disjoint chicken, trim pastry and more.

KNIFE CARE

- To keep knives sharp, cut foods on a soft plastic or wooden cutting board. Ceramic, granite, metal and other hard surfaces will dull the blades.

- Always wash and dry knives by hand immediately after use. Never let them soak in water or wash in the dishwasher.

- Store knives in a slotted wooden block or on a magnetic rack especially designed for knives. Proper storage will protect knife edges, keep blades sharper for longer and guard against injury.

KEEPING SHARP

Rest the tip of the steel on the work surface. Hold your knife at a 20-degree angle to the steel. Start with the heel of the blade against the steel and draw the blade up across the steel until you reach the tip of the knife. Repeat 5 times on both sides of knife blade. Repeat as needed.

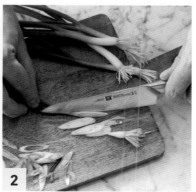

GRIP BASICS

Every cook should master these 2 key grips:

1) Power Grip: Choking up on the knife blade yields more strength and speed for tasks like chopping hard vegetables or cutting through bone.

2) Control Grip: Gently hold the knife handle and treat the blade as an extension of your fingertips for fine, precision tasks.

KITCHEN EQUIPMENT & FOOD SAFETY

Build your collection with the following pieces, then expand to include items as desired from the sidebar on p. 7. The basic pieces for every kitchen include:

BAKEWARE

◄ **13x9-in. baking pan and/or dish (3 qt.)**

► **9x5-in. and 8x4-in. loaf pans**

◄ **15x10x1-in. baking pans**

► **12-cup muffin pan (standard size)**

COOKWARE

◄ **8- or 9-in. saute/ omelet pan**

▲ **1-qt. and 3-qt. saucepans with lids**

◄ **10-in. skillet**

◄ **10- or 12-in. skillet with lid**

► **5- to 8-qt. Dutch oven with lid**

▲ **Roaster with a meat rack**

MEASURING TOOLS

◄ **Liquid measuring cups**

▼ **Dry measuring cups**

► **Measuring spoons**

THERMOMETER

▲ **Thermometer** An instant-read thermometer is a great time-saver and helps you cook with precision. But other styles work fine too.

FOOD SAFETY

To ensure that the food you serve is safe from harmful pathogens, follow these basic but important rules:

KEEP IT CLEAN: Hot, soapy water is a must for hands, knives, work surfaces, cutting boards and utensils used in food preparation. All items, including hands, should be washed before and after touching raw food.

Sanitize cutting boards with a solution of 1 tsp. chlorine bleach to 1 qt. water. Let solution stand on the cutting board several minutes before rinsing clean. Air-dry the board or thoroughly dry it with clean paper towels.

KEEP FOODS SEPARATE: Don't cross-contaminate by allowing the juices or flesh of raw meat to come into contact with other foods. Wash any utensils used in preparation of raw meat in hot, soapy water before using with other foods. Don't reuse packaging materials, such as foam meat trays or plastic wrap.

Also, do not rinse raw poultry, meat or seafood before cooking. Proper cooking will kill any surface bacteria. Washing raw foods will contaminate the sink, which could then transfer bacteria to other foods or utensils if not immediately cleaned and sanitized.

KEEP IT AT THE RIGHT TEMPERATURE: Keep hot foods hot and cold foods cold. Use warming trays and chafing dishes to keep hot foods 140° or higher. Use ice to keep cold food 40° or cooler. Don't keep foods at room temperature for longer than 2 hours (or 1 hour on hot days).

TEMPERATURE DONENESS GUIDELINES

Always cook foods to the proper temperature

TEMPERATURE	WHAT'S COOKING?
135°	Medium-rare: Beef, lamb
140°	Medium: Beef, pork, lamb
140°	Fully cooked ham
145°	Pork, fresh ham (minimum internal temperature)
145°	Medium-well: Beef, lamb
160°	Ground beef, ground pork, ground veal, ground lamb, veal
160°	Egg dishes
165°	Ground chicken, ground turkey, boneless chicken breast, boneless turkey breast, sausages
165°	Casseroles, leftovers, stuffing
170°	Chicken and turkey bone-in breasts, boneless chicken thighs
170°-175°	Whole chicken, whole turkey, bone-in thighs and drumsticks, legs, wings; pheasant
180°	Duck, goose (minimum internal temperature)

EXPANDING YOUR TOOLKIT

Once you have the basic knives, cookware, bakeware, measuring tools and thermometer, consider adding the following items:

- Apple corer
- Blender and/or food processor
- Box grater
- Cake pans (10-in. round)
- Can and bottle opener
- Citrus juicer
- Citrus zester
- Colander
- Corkscrew
- Cutting boards
- Dough cutter/scraper
- Egg slicer
- Ladles, large and small
- Meat fork
- Meat mallet/tenderizer
- Metal skewers
- Metal strainer or sieve
- Mixers, stand or hand
- Mixing bowls
- Mixing spoons
- Pancake turners
- Pastry bags and tips
- Pastry blender
- Pastry brushes
- Pepper mill
- Pie pans
- Pizza cutter
- Potato masher
- Rolling pin
- Salad spinner
- Slotted spoon
- Spatulas, rubber and metal
- Storage and freezer containers
- Thermometers: Candy/deep-fat, oven, refrigerator/freezer
- Textiles: Dishcloths, towels, hot pads, oven mitts
- Tongs
- Utility knife
- Vegetable peeler
- Whisks
- Wire cooling racks

APPS & BEVS

Be the host with the most when you serve these sensational party foods and beverages. From irresistible small bites to dazzling blender drinks, everything you need for the best bash is here.

CHAMPAGNE COCKTAIL

This amber drink is a champagne twist on the traditional old-fashioned. Try it with extra-dry champagne.
—*Taste of Home* Test Kitchen

TAKES: 5 MIN. • **MAKES:** 1 SERVING

  1 **sugar cube or ½ tsp. sugar**
  6 **dashes bitters**
  ½ **oz. brandy**
  ½ **cup chilled champagne**

Optional: Fresh rosemary sprig and fresh or frozen cranberries

Place sugar in a champagne flute or cocktail glass; sprinkle with bitters. Add brandy; top with champagne. If desired, top with rosemary and cranberries.

1 SERVING: 130 cal., 0 fat (0 sat. fat), 0 chol., 0 sod., 5g carb. (2g sugars, 0 fiber), 0 pro.

CHAMPAGNE COCKTAIL TIPS

- **What's the best champagne?** Exceptional champagne can cost a few hundred dollars a bottle, and that's not what you want for a your champagne cocktails. Instead, reach for prosecco, an American bubbly such as Korbel or Gruet, a Spanish cava, or even Asti Spumante from Italy. Remember, the best bubbly wine is the one you prefer. Don't overspend on any wine that you use in a recipe.

- **Is prosecco a champagne?** While Prosecco is delicious, it is not technically champagne. Champagne only comes from Champagne, France. It is made using a procedure that includes a second fermentation in the bottle. (A second fermentation is what makes a wine bubbly). Prosecco, a fun-to-drink Italian wine, undergoes its second fermentation in a large tank. This is called the charmat method. It makes prosecco cheaper to produce than the champagne method, which takes more time and effort.

- **Is champagne stronger than wine?** No. Most champagnes clock in around 11% to 12.5% alcohol, so they are not very strong compared to other types of wines. But there is something tricky about champagne and other fizzy drinks. They tend to go to our heads faster than still (not sparkling) wine or drinks, so it's a good idea to serve and enjoy these alcoholic beverages with food and in moderation.

HOW TO SERVE A BOTTLE OF CHAMPAGNE

Step 1: Remove foil. Look for a tear-strip with a little tab on it, or cut the foil with a wine opener.

Step 2: Carefully remove cage. Untwist the wire loop holding the cage in place on top of the cork. Careful—the cage is what's ensuring the cork stays in the bottle. Once it's loosened or removed, the cork could come out. Point the bottle away from people, your face, and anything fragile.

Step 3: Uncork. Place 1 hand on top of the bottle to help ease out the cork. Gently turn the bottle with your other hand. By controlling how quickly the cork comes out, the result will be a gentle hiss rather than a loud bang.

Step 4: Enjoy! Bubbles last longer if you tilt the glass and gently pour wine against the side of it.

HOLIDAY DEVILED EGGS

Easter:
Top eggs with sprouts. Tuck the ends of a chive into each egg, forming a basket handle. Garnish with candied sunflower kernels.

Halloween:
Use a small and a large straw to cut each egg white into a face with eyes, nose and mouth. Fill whites; dip each finished egg in crushed corn chips.

Christmas:
Add caper eyes, a ham nose and a roasted pepper hat and mouth. With a small star tip, pipe softened cream cheese facial hair and hat trim.

GARLIC-DILL DEVILED EGGS

In my family, Easter isn't complete without deviled eggs. Fresh dill and garlic perk up the flavor of these irresistible appetizers that you'll want to eat on every occasion.
—Kami Horch, Calais, ME

PREP: 20 MIN. + CHILLING
MAKES: 2 DOZEN

- 12 hard-boiled large eggs
- ⅔ cup mayonnaise
- 4 tsp. dill pickle relish
- 2 tsp. snipped fresh dill
- 2 tsp. Dijon mustard
- 1 tsp. coarsely ground pepper
- ¼ tsp. garlic powder
- ⅛ tsp. paprika or cayenne pepper

1. Cut eggs lengthwise in half. Remove yolks, reserving whites. In a bowl, mash yolks. Stir in all remaining ingredients except paprika. Spoon or pipe filling into egg whites.

2. Refrigerate, covered, at least 30 minutes before serving. Sprinkle with paprika.

1 STUFFED EGG HALF: 81 cal., 7g fat (1g sat. fat), 94mg chol., 81mg sod., 1g carb. (0 sugars, 0 fiber), 3g pro.

CRESCENT SAMOSAS

Tender buttery crescents are filled with a delicious filling, making these appetizers a real standout. No one will guess that they're light!
—Jennifer Kemp, Grosse Pointe Park, MI

PREP: 25 MIN. • **BAKE:** 10 MIN. • **MAKES:** 16 APPETIZERS (¾ CUP SAUCE)

¾ cup reduced-fat plain yogurt
2 Tbsp. minced fresh cilantro
1 garlic clove, minced
½ tsp. ground cumin
   Dash pepper

SAMOSAS
1 Tbsp. olive oil
1 can (14½ oz.) diced new potatoes, well drained, or 1¾ cups diced cooked red potatoes

¼ cup canned chopped green chiles
1 garlic clove, minced
1 tsp. curry powder
   Dash pepper
1½ tsp. lemon juice
1 cup frozen peas, thawed
2 tubes (8 oz. each) refrigerated reduced-fat crescent rolls

1. Preheat oven to 375°. For sauce, mix first 5 ingredients; refrigerate until serving.

2. In a large nonstick skillet, heat oil over medium-high heat; saute potatoes until lightly browned. Add chiles, garlic, curry powder and pepper; cook and stir 1 minute. Transfer to a bowl; add lemon juice and coarsely mash. Stir in peas.

3. Unroll crescent dough and separate into 16 triangles. Place 1 Tbsp. potato mixture on the wide end of each triangle; roll up from wide end. Place 2 in. apart on ungreased baking sheets, point side down; curve to form crescents.

4. Bake until golden brown, 10-12 minutes. Serve with sauce.

1 APPETIZER WITH 2 TSP. SAUCE: 130 cal., 6g fat (2g sat. fat), 1mg chol., 305mg sod., 18g carb. (3g sugars, 1g fiber), 4g pro.

SAMOSA SECRETS

The traditional Indian pastry is filled with mashed potatoes, peas, and—of course—a delicious heat from curry powder. Cooling yogurt sauce is a classic accompaniment.

- This quick version calls for canned potatoes, though you could substitute 1¾ cups cooked diced potatoes if preferred.

- For a small-plates party, serve samosas alongside fresh veggies with a creamy dip or a salad containing pink grapefruit or mandarin oranges.

- Make it a feast with Vegan Butter Cauliflower (p.80) or Portobello & Chickpea Sheet-Pan Supper (p. 68).

- Serve refreshing drinks like Old-Fashioned Lemonade or Limeade (p. 18), gin and tonics, or German-style wines such as gewurztraminer or riesling.

RIPEN AVOCADOS QUICKLY

When life hands you hard, less-than-ripe avocados, here's how to ripen them ASAP. Place avocados in a paper bag with an apple or banana. Poke bag a few times with a toothpick or scissors, and let ripen at room temperature 1-2 days. The more fruits you use (and ethylene gas they give off), the faster the results.

GUACAMOLE

This is one of our favorite spicy snack food recipes, and it's quick and easy to prepare when friends drop by on short notice. It also makes a great side dish for a complete southwestern-style meal. Mild or sweet peppers can be substituted for the chiles for those who like their guacamole a little less spicy.
—Anne Tipps, Duncanville, TX

TAKES: 10 MIN. • **MAKES:** ABOUT 1½ CUPS

- 1 medium ripe avocado, halved, seeded and peeled
- 4½ tsp. lemon juice
- 1 small tomato, seeded and finely chopped
- ¼ cup finely chopped red onion
- 1 Tbsp. finely chopped green chiles
- 1 garlic clove, minced
- ¼ tsp. salt, optional
   Tortilla chips

In a large bowl, coarsely mash avocado with lemon juice. Stir in the tomato, onion, chiles, garlic and salt if desired. Cover; chill. Serve with tortilla chips.

2 TBSP.: 29 cal., 3g fat (0 sat. fat), 0 chol., 5mg sod., 2g carb. (1g sugars, 1g fiber), 0 pro.

HOW TO KEEP GUACAMOLE GREEN
It's easy to make your guac ahead of time and keep it nice and green. Just use a thin layer of water to banish browning. Here's how:

Step 1: In an airtight container, use a spoon to flatten the surface of the guacamole and remove any air pockets.

Step 2: Slowly pour in about ½ in. water to cover the surface, using the spoon to gently disperse the water.

Step 3: Refrigerate, covered, up to 2 days. To serve, carefully pour off water, stir guacamole and enjoy.

OLD-FASHIONED LEMONADE

This sweet-tart lemonade is a traditional part of my Memorial Day and Fourth of July menus. Folks can't get enough of the fresh-squeezed flavor.
—Tammi Simpson, Greensburg, KY

PREP: 10 MIN. • **COOK:** 5 MIN. + CHILLING • **MAKES:** 7 SERVINGS

1⅓ cups sugar
5 cups water, divided
1 Tbsp. grated lemon zest

1¾ cups lemon juice (about 10 large lemons)

In a large saucepan, combine sugar, 1 cup water and lemon zest. Cook and stir over medium heat until sugar is dissolved, about 4 minutes. Remove from heat. Stir in lemon juice and remaining water; refrigerate until cold. Serve over ice.

1 CUP: 142 cal., 0 fat (0 sat. fat), 0 chol., 1mg sod., 37g carb. (35g sugars, 0 fiber), 0 pro.

LEMONADE 5 WAYS

- **Limeade:** Substitute lime zest for lemon zest and limes for lemons.

- **Lavender:** Add 2 Tbsp. dried lavender to the sugar and lemon zest mixture before simmering. If desired, strain before serving.

- **Berry:** Substitute 1 cup strained pureed fresh strawberries or raspberries for 1 cup water when making the syrup.

- **Ginger-Mint:** Add 1 Tbsp. grated fresh ginger and ¼ cup fresh mint leaves along with the lemon zest in the syrup. Strain after cooling.

- **SPIKE IT!** For an adults-only version of the kiddie classic, add 1 oz. bourbon or vodka to a tall glass of lemonade. Rim the glass with sugar for an extra-fancy cocktail.

BERRY

LAVENDER

GINGER-MINT

KEEP IT COOL

Freeze extra lemon slices, covered with lemonade or water, in ice cube trays. They'll look pretty and cool your drink without diluting it.

FRUIT COMPOTE WITH BRIE

This yummy compote is so versatile. I stir it into yogurt or serve it over cheesecake, ice cream, blintzes and crepes. And of course, it makes Brie taste amazing!
—Clara Coulson Minney, Washington Court House, OH

TAKES: 15 MIN. • **MAKES:** 8 SERVINGS

1	round (8 oz.) Brie cheese	1	tsp. vanilla extract
⅔	cup golden raisins and cherries	1	Tbsp. cherry preserves
⅓	cup unsweetened apple juice		Assorted crackers

1. Preheat oven to 400°. Place cheese on a small ungreased cast-iron skillet or shallow 1-qt. baking dish. Bake until cheese is softened, 8-10 minutes.

2. Meanwhile, in a small saucepan, combine the golden raisins and cherries, apple juice and vanilla; bring to a boil. Remove from the heat; stir in preserves. Spoon over cheese. Serve with crackers.

1 SERVING: 140 cal., 8g fat (5g sat. fat), 28mg chol., 179mg sod., 11g carb. (9g sugars, 1g fiber), 6g pro.

EVERYBODY LOVES BRIE

Buttery and with an edible, slightly salty rind, Brie cheese is ideal for pairing with a fruity compote.

For a quick serving idea or a picnic, team up Brie with sliced apples or pears, baguette slices and/or water crackers.

You can substitute Camembert in any recipe that calls for Brie. For a flavorful treat, look for St. Andre, a French cheese that is even richer and creamier than Brie. (It's a triple-cream cheese, while Brie and Camembert are "only" double-cream.) But they're all heavenly!

FROZEN MARGARITAS

One of my favorite summer drinks is a frozen margarita. What's not to love? This drink is great paired with tacos or chips and salsa.
—Caroline Stanko, Milwaukee, WI

TAKES: 15 MIN. • **MAKES:** 6 SERVINGS

6 lime wedges
  Kosher salt
1 cup tequila
½ cup Triple Sec
¼ cup lime juice (about 4 limes)
½ cup simple syrup or super fine sugar
6 to 9 cups ice cubes

1. Using lime wedges, moisten the rims of 6 margarita or cocktail glasses. Set aside lime wedges for garnish. Sprinkle salt on a plate; hold each glass upside down and dip rim into salt. Set aside. Discard remaining salt on plate.

2. In a blender, combine the tequila, Triple Sec, lime juice, simple syrup and enough ice to reach desired consistency; cover and process until blended. Pour into prepared glasses. Garnish with lime wedges. Serve margaritas immediately.

1 CUP: 214 cal., 0 fat (0 sat. fat), 0 chol., 34mg sod., 24g carb. (22g sugars, 0 fiber), 0 pro.

MARGARITA ON THE ROCKS

Combine 1½ oz. blanco tequila, 1 oz. orange liqueur and ½ oz. fresh-squeezed lime juice in a cocktail shaker, then fill glass three-fourths full with ice. Cover and shake until the outside of shaker is frosted, about 20 seconds.

To salt rims: Rub a slice of lime around the rim of your margarita glass, then roll the rim in a plate of salt until it's coated in salt.

GIVE THESE FLAVORS A WHIRL

1) Raspberry-Ginger Margarita: In a blender, mix 1 cup frozen raspberries, 1½ oz. blanco tequila, 1 oz. ginger liqueur, 1 oz. raspberry liqueur and ½ oz. freshly squeezed lime juice. Garnish: Sugared rim, raspberry and crystallized ginger.

2) Coconut Margarita: In a blender, mix 1 cup crushed ice, 2 oz. cream of coconut, 1½ oz. blanco tequila, 1 oz. Triple Sec and ½ oz. fresh lime juice. Garnish: Chopped toasted shredded coconut on rim and toasted coconut.

CRUMB-TOPPED CLAMS

In my family, it wouldn't be Christmas Eve without baked clams. However, they make a special bite for any occasion and are easy to make and always a hit.
—Annmarie Lucente, Monroe, NY

PREP: 35 MIN. • **BROIL:** 10 MIN. • **MAKES:** 2 DOZEN

2 lbs. kosher salt
2 dozen fresh littleneck clams
½ cup dry bread crumbs
¼ cup chicken broth
1 Tbsp. minced fresh parsley
2 Tbsp. olive oil
2 garlic cloves, minced
¼ tsp. dried oregano
   Dash pepper
1 Tbsp. panko bread crumbs
   Lemon wedges

1. Spread salt onto a cast-iron 15x10x1-in. baking pan or other ovenproof metal serving plater. Shuck clams, leaving clams and juices in bottom shells. Arrange in prepared platter; divide juices among shells.

2. In a small bowl, mix dry bread crumbs, chicken broth, parsley, oil, garlic, oregano and pepper; spoon over clams. Sprinkle with panko bread crumbs.

3. Broil 4-6 in. from heat until clams are firm and crumb mixture is crisp and golden brown, 6-8 minutes. Serve immediately with lemon wedges.

1 CLAM: 31 cal., 1g fat (0 sat. fat), 5mg chol., 35mg sod., 2g carb. (0 sugars, 0 fiber), 2g pro.

HOW TO SHUCK A HARD-SHELL CLAM

Step 1: Scrub under cold running water with a stiff brush. Place on a tray and chill 30 minutes (they'll be easier to open).

Step 2: Protect your hand by placing the clam in a clean kitchen towel with the hinge facing out. Insert clam knife next to the hinge. Slide the knife around to loosen the shells.

Step 3: Open the top shell and cut away the muscle from the top shell. Discard the top shell.

Step 4: Use the knife to release the clam from the bottom shell. If desired, pour clam juice into a strainer and reserve for your recipe.

ANTIPASTO PLATTER

We entertain often, and antipasto is one of our favorite crowd-pleasers. Guests love having their choice of so many delicious nibbles, including pepperoni and cubes of provolone.
—Teri Lindquist, Gurnee, IL

PREP: 10 MIN. + CHILLING • **MAKES:** 16 SERVINGS (4 QT.)

1 jar (24 oz.) pepperoncini, drained
1 can (15 oz.) garbanzo beans or chickpeas, rinsed and drained
2 cups halved fresh mushrooms
2 cups halved cherry tomatoes
½ lb. provolone cheese, cubed
1 can (6 oz.) pitted ripe olives, drained
1 pkg. (3½ oz.) sliced pepperoni
1 bottle (8 oz.) Italian vinaigrette dressing
Lettuce leaves

1. In a large bowl, combine pepperoncini, beans, mushrooms, tomatoes, cheese, olives and pepperoni. Pour vinaigrette over mixture; toss to coat.

2. Refrigerate at least 30 minutes or overnight. Arrange on a lettuce-lined platter. Serve with toothpicks.

1 CUP: 178 cal., 13g fat (4g sat. fat), 15mg chol., 852mg sod., 8g carb. (2g sugars, 2g fiber), 6g pro.

TEST KITCHEN TIPS

• Be sure to make this ahead. The flavor gets better as it sits!

• Toss leftover antipasto with salad greens or cooked, cooled cheese tortellini for a quick lunch.

ANTIPASTO INSIGHTS

Loosely meaning "before the pasta" in Italian, antipasto is a delightful and satisfying first course, perfect for grazing. Mix it up to include your own favorites; there are no rules. Consider these:

• Salami, sopressata or other Italian deli meats

• Fresh mozzarella cheese pearls or traditional (in a block form) mozzarella or pecorino, cut into small cubes

• Roasted red peppers or pickled cherry peppers

• A blend of olives from your grocery store's olive bar

• Seasoned zucchini or eggplant that you've grilled yourself

• Marinated artichokes

• Grape or pear tomatoes, tossed with oil and broiled until blistered

• Pickled garlic

• Chopped sun-dried tomatoes, basil or parsley

ABOUT
SPRING ROLLS

- Thin and delicate spring roll wrappers are like super thin crepes made from rice flour and tapioca flour.

- To soften wrappers, dip them briefly in water and work with 1 at a time.

- The spring rolls may be made in advance; just cover with damp paper towels to keep them moist and refrigerate in a covered container.

- Spring rolls (made with the season's first spring vegetables) are a classic dish for Chinese New Year.

PORK & VEGETABLE SPRING ROLLS

I thought rice paper wrappers would be a quick, fun way to put salad ingredients into a hand-held snack. I also make these spring rolls with shrimp and dried cranberries. Go ahead, experiment!
—Marla Strader, Ozark, MO

TAKES: 30 MIN. • **MAKES:** 4 SERVINGS

- 2 cups thinly sliced romaine
- 1½ cups cubed cooked pork
- 1 cup thinly sliced fresh spinach
- ¾ cup julienned carrot
- ⅓ cup thinly sliced celery
- ⅓ cup dried cherries, coarsely chopped
- 1 Tbsp. sesame oil
- 12 round rice paper wrappers (8 in.)
- ¼ cup sliced almonds
- ¼ cup wasabi-coated green peas
  Sesame ginger salad dressing

1. In a large bowl, combine the first 6 ingredients. Drizzle with oil; toss to coat.

2. Fill a large shallow dish partway with water. Dip a rice paper wrapper into water just until pliable, about 45 seconds (do not soften completely); allow excess water to drip off.

3. Place wrapper on a flat surface. Layer salad mixture, almonds and peas across bottom third of wrapper. Fold in both ends of wrapper; fold bottom side over filling, then roll up tightly. Place on a serving plate, seam side down. Repeat with remaining ingredients. Serve with dressing.

3 SPRING ROLLS: 255 cal., 12g fat (3g sat. fat), 48mg chol., 91mg sod., 19g carb. (10g sugars, 3g fiber), 18g pro. **DIABETIC EXCHANGES:** 3 lean meat, 1 starch, 1 vegetable, 1 fat.

PERFECT LEMON MARTINI

Relax with a refreshing cocktail. This combo of tart lemon and sweet liqueur will tingle your taste buds.
—Marilee Anker, Chatsworth, CA

TAKES: 5 MIN. • **MAKES:** 1 SERVING

1	lemon slice	2	oz. vodka
	Sugar	1½	oz. limoncello
	Ice cubes	½	oz. lemon juice

Using lemon slice, moisten the rim of a chilled cocktail glass; set lemon aside. Sprinkle sugar on a plate; hold glass upside down and dip rim into sugar. Discard remaining sugar on plate. Fill a shaker three-fourths full with ice. Add vodka, limoncello and lemon juice; cover and shake until condensation forms on outside of shaker, 10-15 seconds. Strain into prepared glass. Garnish with lemon slice.

1 SERVING: 286 cal., 0 fat (0 sat. fat), 0 chol., 1mg sod., 18g carb. (17g sugars, 0 fiber), 0 pro.

LIMONCELLO SPRITZER

Fill a wine glass with ice. Squeeze a lemon wedge over ice; drop lemon into the glass. Pour in ½ cup chilled club soda and 1 oz. each of vodka and limoncello. Stir.

HOW TO MAKE LIMONCELLO

Makes: 6 cups

You'll need:
- 10 medium lemons
- 1 bottle (750 ml) vodka
- 3 cups water
- 1½ cups sugar

Step 1: Using a vegetable peeler, peel rind from lemons (save lemons for another use). With a sharp knife, scrape pith from peels and discard. Place lemon peels and vodka in a large glass or plastic container. Cover and let stand at room temperature for at least 2 weeks, stirring once a week.

Step 2: In a large saucepan, bring water and sugar to a boil. Reduce heat; simmer, uncovered, for 10 minutes. Cool completely.

Step 3: Strain vodka mixture, discarding lemon peels. Return mixture to container; stir in sugar mixture. Pour into glass bottles; seal tightly. Let stand 2 weeks. Serve cold.

BUFFALO WING SAUCE

SPICY THAI SAUCE

SPICY BARBECUE SAUCE

HOW TO CUT CHICKEN WINGS

Step 1: Place chicken wing on a cutting board. With a sharp knife, cut through the joint at the tip end.

Step 2: Cut through remaining wing joint, creating a wingette and drumette. Repeat with remaining wings.

BEST EVER FRIED CHICKEN WINGS

For game days, I shake up these saucy wings. When I run out, friends hover by the snack table until I bring out more. When they ask me how to fry chicken wings, they never believe it's so easy!
—Nick Iverson, Denver, CO

PREP: 10 MIN. + CHILLING • **COOK:** 20 MIN. • **MAKES:** ABOUT 4 DOZEN

4 lbs. chicken wings
2 tsp. kosher salt
   Oil for deep-fat frying

BUFFALO WING SAUCE
¾ cup Louisiana-style hot sauce
¼ cup unsalted butter, cubed
2 Tbsp. molasses
¼ tsp. cayenne pepper

SPICY THAI SAUCE
1 Tbsp. canola oil
1 tsp. grated fresh gingerroot
1 garlic clove, minced
1 minced Thai chile pepper or ¼ tsp. crushed red pepper flakes
¼ cup packed dark brown sugar
2 Tbsp. lime juice
2 Tbsp. minced fresh cilantro
1 Tbsp. fish sauce

SPICY BARBECUE SAUCE
¾ cup barbecue sauce
2 chipotle peppers in adobo sauce, finely chopped
2 Tbsp. honey
1 Tbsp. cider vinegar

1. Using a sharp knife, cut through the 2 wing joints; discard wing tips. Pat chicken dry with paper towels. Toss wings with kosher salt. Place on a wire rack in a 15x10x1-in. baking pan. Refrigerate at least 1 hour or overnight.

2. In an electric skillet or deep-fat fryer, heat oil to 375°. Fry wings in batches until skin is crisp and meat is tender, 8-10 minutes. Drain on paper towels.

3. For Buffalo wing sauce, bring the hot sauce just to a boil in a small saucepan. Remove from heat; whisk in butter 1 piece at a time. Stir in molasses and cayenne pepper.

4. For Thai sauce, heat oil in a small saucepan over medium heat. Add ginger, garlic and chile pepper; cook and stir until fragrant, about 2 minutes. Stir in brown sugar and lime juice. Bring to a boil; cook until slightly thickened, about 5 minutes. Stir in cilantro and fish sauce.

5. For barbecue sauce, heat the prepared barbecue sauce in a small saucepan over medium heat. Stir in chipotle peppers, honey and vinegar. Bring to a boil; cook and stir until slightly thickened, about 5 minutes.

6. Toss wings with the sauce of your choice.

1 PIECE WITH BUFFALO WING SAUCE: 87 cal., 8g fat (2g sat. fat), 15mg chol., 218mg sod., 1g carb. (1g sugars, 0 fiber), 4g pro. **1 PIECE WITH SPICY THAI SAUCE:** 82 cal., 7g fat (1g sat. fat), 12mg chol., 121mg sod., 1g carb. (1g sugars, 0 fiber), 4g pro. **1 PIECE WITH SPICY BARBECUE SAUCE:** 85 cal., 7g fat (1g sat. fat), 12mg chol., 136mg sod., 2g carb. (1g sugars, 0 fiber), 4g pro.

AIR-FRIED VARIATION

Preheat air fryer to 400°. Spray air-fryer basket with cooking spray. Working in batches, place wings in a single layer in basket. Cook 6 minutes; turn and brush with sauce mixture. Return to air fryer and cook until browned and juices run clear, 6-8 minutes longer. Remove and keep warm. Repeat with remaining wings.

THREE-CHEESE FONDUE

I got this easy recipe from my daughter, who lives in France. It's become my go-to fondue, and I make it often for our family.
—Betty Mangas, Toledo, OH

TAKES: 30 MIN. • **MAKES:** 4 CUPS

2 cups dry white wine
4 tsp. cherry brandy
2 Tbsp. cornstarch
⅛ tsp. ground nutmeg
⅛ tsp. paprika
    Dash cayenne pepper
½ lb. each Emmenthaler, Gruyere and Jarlsberg cheeses, finely shredded
    Cubed French bread baguette, boiled red potatoes and/or tiny whole pickles

1. In a large saucepan, whisk together first 6 ingredients until smooth. Heat the mixture over medium heat until slightly thickened, stirring constantly, 5-7 minutes.

2. Reduce heat to low; gradually add ½ cup cheese, stirring constantly with a figure-eight motion, until cheese is melted (cheese will separate from wine mixture). Gradually add remaining cheese, allowing cheese to melt between additions. Cook and stir until thickened and mixture is blended and smooth, 4-5 minutes.

3. Transfer to a fondue pot and keep warm. Serve with bread cubes, potatoes and/or pickles.

¼ CUP: 191 cal., 12g fat (7g sat. fat), 37mg chol., 151mg sod., 3g carb. (1g sugars, 0 fiber), 12g pro.

SOUPS

Yes, you can master old-fashioned dumplings, homemade bone broth, chicken stock and traditional gumbo. Brush up on chowder, chicken noodle and restaurant-style favorites too.

SHRIMP GUMBO

Serve a crisp green salad and crusty French bread to make this shrimp gumbo a complete meal. I always have hot sauce available when I prepare this so people can customize the heat level.
—Jo Ann Graham, Ovilla, TX

PREP: 30 MIN. • **COOK:** 1 HOUR • **MAKES:** 11 SERVINGS (2¾ QT.)

¼ cup all-purpose flour
¼ cup canola oil
3 celery ribs, chopped
1 medium green pepper, chopped
1 medium onion, chopped
4 cups chicken broth
3 garlic cloves, minced
1 tsp. salt
1 tsp. pepper
½ tsp. cayenne pepper
2 lbs. uncooked shrimp (26-30 per lb.), peeled and deveined
1 pkg. (16 oz.) frozen sliced okra
4 green onions, sliced
1 medium tomato, chopped
1½ tsp. gumbo file powder
Hot cooked rice

1. In a Dutch oven over medium heat, cook and stir flour and oil until caramel-colored, stirring occasionally, about 12 minutes (do not burn). Add the celery, green pepper and onion; cook and stir until tender, 5-6 minutes. Stir in the broth, garlic, salt, pepper and cayenne; bring to a boil. Reduce heat; cover and simmer for 30 minutes.

2. Stir in the shrimp, okra, green onions and tomato. Return to a boil. Reduce heat; cover and simmer until shrimp turn pink, about 10 minutes. Stir in file powder. Serve with rice.

1 CUP: 159 cal., 7g fat (1g sat. fat), 102mg chol., 681mg sod., 9g carb. (3g sugars, 2g fiber), 15g pro. **DIABETIC EXCHANGES:** 2 lean meat, 1 vegetable, 1 fat.

TEST KITCHEN TIP

Gumbo file powder, used to thicken and flavor Creole recipes, is available in spice shops. If you don't want to use gumbo file powder, combine 2 Tbsp. each of cornstarch and water until smooth. Gradually stir into gumbo. Bring to a boil; cook and stir for 2 minutes or until thickened.

ROUX STAGES

1) White. Add equal parts flour and oil or butter to a cast-iron skillet over medium heat; stir to combine.

2) Blonde. Continue cooking over medium heat, stirring occasionally.

3) Brown. Mixture will begin to brown after first 10 minutes of cooking. Continue cooking over medium heat, stirring occasionally, until mixture is caramel-colored.

4) Dark. Continue cooking over medium heat until mixture is dark brown. Stir constantly to avoid burning.

COOKING WITH ROUX

Roux (pronounced *roo*) is what makes chowders and stews thick and silky smooth. It's what makes gumbos rich and nutty. And—believe it or not—it's made up of just 2 ingredients. Stirred into hundreds of recipes, a roux is a mixture of equal parts flour and fat, oftentimes butter or oil. There are many kinds, all with the same 2 elements but differentiated by their colors and cook times.

- **White Roux:** This is the most common and has the most thickening power. Cook it just long enough to eliminate the flour's raw flavor, 2-3 minutes.

- **Blonde Roux:** This has an off-white color similar to eggshell and a buttery flavor. It's perfect for thickening quick pan sauces. Cook it 5-10 minutes. (Psst! You can use this roux in any recipe that calls for a white roux too.)

- **Brown Roux:** This is caramel-colored and has a nutty, rich flavor. Use it in ethnic soups and stews, and cook it for 20-30 minutes.

- **Dark Roux:** This is the darkest and most flavorful; it requires constant stirring. Most brown roux use vegetable oil instead of butter. Cook at least 45 minutes.

WATCH US MAKE IT
Just hover your camera here.

ZIPPY CHICKEN & CORN CHOWDER

Gently spiced corn chowder is always a good option for kids, but adults can rev up their servings with hot pepper sauce. This soup is my go-to on busy nights.
—Andrea Early, Harrisonburg, VA

PREP: 15 MIN. • **COOK:** 25 MIN. • **MAKES:** 8 SERVINGS (3 QT.)

¼ **cup butter**
1 **large onion, chopped**
1 **medium green pepper, chopped**
¼ **cup all-purpose flour**
1 **Tbsp. paprika**
2 **medium potatoes, peeled and chopped**
1 **carton (32 oz.) chicken broth**
1 **skinned rotisserie chicken, shredded**
6 **cups fresh or frozen corn**
1 **Tbsp. Worcestershire sauce**
½ **to 1 tsp. hot pepper sauce**
1 **tsp. salt**
1 **cup 2% milk**

1. In a stockpot, heat butter over medium-high heat. Add onion and pepper; cook and stir until vegetables are crisp-tender, 3-4 minutes. Stir in flour and paprika until blended.

2. Add potatoes; stir in broth. Bring to a boil; reduce heat and simmer, covered, until tender, 12-15 minutes.

3. Stir in chicken, corn, sauces and salt; bring to a boil. Reduce heat and cook, uncovered, until corn is tender, 4-6 minutes. Add milk; heat through (do not boil).

1½ CUPS: 351 cal., 12g fat (5g sat. fat), 75mg chol., 920mg sod., 39g carb. (7g sugars, 4g fiber), 25g pro.

TRY IT 3 NEW WAYS

- **Cajun Chicken & Shrimp Chowder:** Make chowder as directed. Add a half-pound of shrimp and Cajun seasoning. Serve with additional hot pepper sauce and crackers.

- **Buffalo Chicken Chowder:** Make as directed. Add more hot pepper sauce. Top with blue cheese crumbles and a ranch dressing drizzle.

- **Succotash-Style Chowder:** Make as directed. Add lima beans, crumbled bacon and halved cherry tomatoes.

HOMEMADE CHICKEN STOCK

Rich in chicken flavor, this traditional stock is lightly seasoned with herbs. Besides making wonderful chicken soups, it can be used in casseroles, rice dishes and other recipes that call for chicken broth.
—*Taste of Home* Test Kitchen

PREP: 10 MIN. • **COOK:** 3¼ HOURS + CHILLING • **MAKES:** ABOUT 6 CUPS

- 2½ lbs. bony chicken pieces (legs, wings, necks or back bones)
- 2 celery ribs with leaves, cut into chunks
- 2 medium carrots, cut into chunks
- 2 medium onions, quartered
- 2 bay leaves
- ½ tsp. dried rosemary, crushed
- ½ tsp. dried thyme
- 8 to 10 whole peppercorns
- 2 qt. cold water

1. Place all ingredients in a soup kettle or Dutch oven. Slowly bring to a boil; reduce heat until mixture is just at a simmer. Simmer, uncovered, for 3-4 hours, skimming foam as necessary.

2. Set chicken aside until cool enough to handle. Remove meat from bones. Discard bones; save meat for another use. Strain broth, discarding vegetables and seasonings. Cool. Refrigerate for 8 hours or overnight. Skim fat from surface.

1 CUP: 25 cal., 0 fat (0 sat. fat), 0 chol., 130mg sod., 2g carb. (0 sugars, 0 fiber), 4g pro.

TEST KITCHEN TIP

To give limp celery a second chance for use in recipes, cut the ends from the stalks and place the stalks in a glass of cold water. Let stand in the refrigerator for several hours or overnight. You'll be surprised how refreshed the celery will be.

CHICKEN STOCK SUCCESS TIPS

- Keep the liquid at a bare and steady simmer (not a full rolling boil). This helps impurities rise to the top, which you can skim off as foam. Skimming the foam ensures a clear and well-flavored—not cloudy—broth.

- The longer you simmer your stock, the more collagen is extracted, giving the finished liquid a rich and silky texture.

- The terms "stock" and "broth" are often interchanged by chefs and home cooks. To be 100% accurate, the term stock refers to liquid made from bones, fat, meat and vegetables. Broth is made with just meat and vegetables. Stock is what most people are preparing when they make this flavorful liquid at home.

- Most stocks and broths can be frozen for up to a year in sealed containers.

CASSOULET FOR TODAY

Traditionally cooked for hours, this version of the rustic French cassoulet offers the same homey taste in less time. It's easy on the wallet too.
—Virginia C. Anthony, Jacksonville, FL

PREP: 45 MIN. • **BAKE:** 50 MIN. • **MAKES:** 6 SERVINGS

6 boneless skinless chicken thighs (about 1½ lbs.)
¼ tsp. salt
¼ tsp. coarsely ground pepper
3 tsp. olive oil, divided
1 large onion, chopped
1 garlic clove, minced
½ cup white wine or chicken broth
1 can (14½ oz.) diced tomatoes, drained
1 bay leaf
1 tsp. minced fresh rosemary or ¼ tsp. dried rosemary, crushed
1 tsp. minced fresh thyme or ¼ tsp. dried thyme
2 cans (15 oz. each) cannellini beans, rinsed and drained
¼ lb. smoked turkey kielbasa, chopped
3 bacon strips, cooked and crumbled

TOPPING
½ cup soft whole wheat bread crumbs
¼ cup minced fresh parsley
1 garlic clove, minced

1. Preheat oven to 325°. Sprinkle the chicken with salt and pepper. In a broiler-safe Dutch oven, heat 2 tsp. oil over medium heat; brown chicken on both sides. Remove from pan.

2. In same pan, saute the onion in remaining oil over medium heat until crisp-tender. Add garlic; cook 1 minute. Add wine; bring to a boil, stirring to loosen browned bits from pan. Add tomatoes, herbs and chicken; return to a boil.

3. Transfer to oven; bake, covered, 30 minutes. Stir in beans and kielbasa; bake, covered, until chicken is tender, 20-25 minutes longer.

4. Remove from oven; preheat broiler. Discard bay leaf; stir in bacon. Toss bread crumbs with parsley and garlic; sprinkle over top. Place in oven so surface of cassoulet is 4-5 in. from heat; broil until crumbs are golden brown, 2-3 minutes.

1 SERVING: 394 cal., 14g fat (4g sat. fat), 91mg chol., 736mg sod., 29g carb. (4g sugars, 8g fiber), 33g pro. **DIABETIC EXCHANGES:** 4 lean meat, 2 starch, ½ fat.

HEALTH TIP

Adding pulses such as beans to a meat-based main dish bumps up the fiber and protein without adding saturated fat.

CASSOULET: A CLASSIC, VERSATILE STEW

Pronounced *KASS-soo-LAY*, this southern French stew traditionally contains white beans and a variety of meats (including duck, goose, pork, lamb and sausages).

Our lightened-up version uses leaner meats and isn't thickened with a butter-and-flour roux (learn more on p. 39). For a richer taste, you could prepare this recipe with 2 Tbsp. each butter and flour cooked to a brown-roux stage, before adding the wine and tomatoes.

Serve cassoulet with a green salad and your favorite crusty bread for an informal fall get-together.

To stretch this recipe, increase the smoked sausage or beans, stir in cubed cooked pork, or simmer along with some chicken or duck legs.

Pinot noir and chardonnay would go excellently here. If your gang prefers red wine, go ahead and use it in the stew instead of white wine. Cassoulet is a flexible, forgiving dish!

GARDEN VEGETABLE & HERB SOUP

I submitted this recipe to a local newspaper and won first prize. I make this hearty soup whenever my family needs a good dose of veggies.
—Jody Saulnier, North Woodstock, NH

PREP: 20 MIN. • **COOK:** 30 MIN. • **MAKES:** 8 SERVINGS (2 QT.)

2 Tbsp. olive oil
2 medium onions, chopped
2 large carrots, sliced
1 lb. red potatoes (about 3 medium), cubed
2 cups water
1 can (14½ oz.) diced tomatoes in sauce
1½ cups vegetable broth
1½ tsp. garlic powder
1 tsp. dried basil
½ tsp. salt
½ tsp. paprika
¼ tsp. dill weed
¼ tsp. pepper
1 medium yellow summer squash, halved and sliced
1 medium zucchini, halved and sliced

1. In a large saucepan, heat oil over medium heat. Add onions and carrots; cook and stir until onions are tender, 4-6 minutes. Add potatoes and cook 2 minutes. Stir in water, tomatoes, broth and seasonings. Bring to a boil. Reduce heat; simmer, uncovered, until potatoes and carrots are tender, 8-10 minutes.

2. Add yellow squash and zucchini; cook until vegetables are tender, 8-10 minutes longer. Serve or, if desired, puree mixture in batches, adding additional broth until desired consistency is achieved.

1 CUP: 115 cal., 4g fat (1g sat. fat), 0 chol., 525mg sod., 19g carb. (6g sugars, 3g fiber), 2g pro. **DIABETIC EXCHANGES:** 1 vegetable, 1 fat, ½ starch.

BLENDED SOUP SUCCESS

Left chunky or pureed until smooth, vegetable soups are healthful way to eat more veggies. Blending the soup in a traditional pitcher-style blender, as shown, will create a smoother, silkier texture than an immersion blender would. If you want to save time and dishes (and don't mind a more rustic texture), you could use an immersion blender right in the soup pot instead.

BUILD FLAVOR WITH CARAMELIZED ONIONS

Coax every little bit of flavor from a heap of onions for this melty, cheesy soup du jour. You'll be whisked away to a Paris cafe without having to leave your kitchen.

Pick your fave

Almost any onion variety will give you the rich flavor of this classic soup. Try Spanish, yellow or white onions—leeks will work too—but use sweet onions sparingly, as their sweetness can overpower the finished product.

Low & slow

Patience is key—if you brown the onions too quickly, you won't extract the natural sugars, and the soup will end up thin, flat and boring. For intense flavor, cook the onions over low heat for a long time, stirring often.

Freeze it

Caramelized onions freeze beautifully, so why not double the batch and store half for a future meal? You can freeze the completely cooked soup for up to 6 months. Just omit the bread and cheese, let cool and freeze.

CLASSIC FRENCH ONION SOUP

Enjoy my signature soup the way my granddaughter Becky does: I make it for her in a French onion soup bowl complete with garlic croutons and gobs of melted Swiss cheese on top.
—Lou Sansevero, Ferron, UT

PREP: 20 MIN. • **COOK:** 2 HOURS • **MAKES:** 12 SERVINGS (2¼ QT.)

5 Tbsp. olive oil, divided
1 Tbsp. butter
8 cups thinly sliced onions (about 3 lbs.)
3 garlic cloves, minced
½ cup port wine
2 cartons (32 oz. each) beef broth
½ tsp. pepper
¼ tsp. salt
24 slices French bread baguette (½ in. thick)
2 large garlic cloves, peeled and halved
¾ cup shredded Gruyere or Swiss cheese

1. In a Dutch oven, heat 2 Tbsp. oil and butter over medium heat. Add onions; cook and stir until softened, 10-13 minutes. Reduce heat to medium-low; cook, stirring occasionally, until deep golden brown, 30-40 minutes. Add minced garlic; cook 2 minutes longer.

2. Stir in wine. Bring to a boil; cook until liquid is reduced by half. Add broth, pepper and salt; return to a boil. Reduce heat. Simmer, covered, stirring occasionally, for 1 hour.

3. Meanwhile, preheat oven to 400°. Place baguette slices on a baking sheet; brush both sides with remaining 3 Tbsp. oil. Bake until toasted, 3-5 minutes on each side. Rub toasts with halved garlic.

4. To serve, place twelve 8-oz. broiler-safe bowls or ramekins on baking sheets; place 2 toasts in each. Ladle with soup; top with cheese. Broil 4 in. from heat until cheese is melted.

¾ CUP SOUP WITH 2 SLICES BREAD AND 1 TBSP. CHEESE: 195 cal., 10g fat (3g sat. fat), 9mg chol., 805mg sod., 20g carb. (4g sugars, 2g fiber), 6g pro.

THE ULTIMATE CHICKEN NOODLE SOUP

My first Wisconsin winter was so cold, all I wanted to eat was soup. This recipe is in heavy rotation at our house from November to April.
—Gina Nistico, Denver, CO

PREP: 15 MIN. • **COOK:** 45 MIN. + STANDING • **MAKES:** 10 SERVINGS (ABOUT 3½ QT.)

2½ lbs. bone-in chicken thighs
½ tsp. salt
½ tsp. pepper
1 Tbsp. canola oil
1 large onion, chopped
1 garlic clove, minced
10 cups chicken broth
4 celery ribs, chopped
4 medium carrots, chopped
2 bay leaves
1 tsp. minced fresh thyme or ¼ tsp. dried thyme
3 cups uncooked kluski or other egg noodles (about 8 oz.)
1 Tbsp. chopped fresh parsley
1 Tbsp. lemon juice
Optional: Additional salt and pepper

1. Pat chicken dry with paper towels; sprinkle with salt and pepper. In a 6-qt. stockpot, heat oil over medium-high heat. Add chicken in batches, skin side down; cook until dark golden brown, 3-4 minutes. Remove chicken from pan; remove and discard skin. Discard all but 2 Tbsp. drippings.

2. Add onion to drippings; cook and stir over medium-high heat until tender, 4-5 minutes. Add garlic; cook 1 minute longer. Add broth, stirring to loosen browned bits from pan. Bring to a boil. Return chicken to pan. Add celery, carrots, bay leaves and thyme. Reduce heat; simmer, covered, until chicken is tender, 25-30 minutes.

3. Transfer chicken to a plate. Remove soup from heat. Add noodles; let stand, covered, until noodles are tender, 20-22 minutes.

4. Meanwhile, when chicken is cool enough to handle, remove meat from bones; discard bones. Shred meat into bite-sized pieces. Return meat to stockpot. Stir in parsley and lemon juice. If desired, adjust seasoning with additional salt and pepper. Discard bay leaves.

1⅓ CUPS: 239 cal., 12g fat (3g sat. fat), 68mg chol., 1176mg sod., 14g carb. (3g sugars, 2g fiber), 18g pro.

HOW TO FIX THE BIGGEST CHICKEN SOUP PROBLEMS

- **Mushy noodles.** To prevent soggy noodles, let the uncooked egg noodles stand in the hot soup, covered, for 20 minutes before serving. Cooking the noodles off-heat ensures they plump gently; doing so in the soup means they absorb the delicious broth instead of boring ol' water.

- **Dry, tasteless chicken.** Say buh-bye to blah chicken by opting for bone-in thighs instead. They stay juicy and moist, with a richer and more robust flavor than boneless skinless chicken breasts.

- **Bland broth.** The thighs are key here, too. Give a homey boost to store-bought broth by searing meaty, skin-on chicken thighs first. This builds those irresistible brown bits on the bottom of the pan before you add the broth. A little spritz of lemon juice is the finishing touch. The subtle contrast brightens and balances the herby, savory broth.

HOW TO KEEP CHICKEN TENDER

To prevent your chicken from drying out, remove it from the broth when tender. Let cool, shred and set aside while you finish making the soup. Then return the chicken to the hot soup when you're ready to eat.

SEE THE 1-MINUTE VERSION
Just hover your camera here..

HOW TO DESTEM KALE

Fold a washed kale leaf in half. For smaller leaves, use fingers to tear kale from the tough stem. For large leaves, cut the stem away with a large chef's knife. Chop kale as desired.

POTATO, SAUSAGE & KALE SOUP

I let my young son pick out seed packets for our garden and he chose kale, which grew like crazy. This hearty soup helped make good use of it and rivals the Olive Garden's zuppa Toscana.
—Michelle Babbie, Malone, NY

TAKES: 30 MIN. • **MAKES:** 4 SERVINGS

½ **lb. bulk pork sausage**
1 **medium onion, finely chopped**
2 **tsp. chicken bouillon granules**
½ **tsp. garlic powder**
½ **tsp. pepper**
2 **medium red potatoes, cut into ½-in. cubes**
2 **cups sliced fresh kale**
3 **cups 2% milk**
1 **cup heavy whipping cream**
1 **Tbsp. cornstarch**
¼ **cup cold water**

1. In a large saucepan, cook sausage and onion over medium heat 4-6 minutes or until sausage is no longer pink and onion is tender, breaking up sausage into crumbles; drain.

2. Stir in seasonings. Add potatoes, kale, milk and cream; bring to a boil. Reduce heat; simmer, covered, 10-15 minutes or until potatoes are tender.

3. In a small bowl, mix cornstarch and water until smooth; stir into soup. Return to a boil, stirring constantly; cook and stir 1-2 minutes or until thickened.

1½ CUPS: 504 cal., 38g fat (20g sat. fat), 128mg chol., 881mg sod., 26g carb. (12g sugars, 2g fiber), 15g pro.

CHOWDER, DEFINED

This hearty soup contains the 3 key ingredients of classic chowder: pork (in the form of sausage), potatoes and dairy. Increasingly, "chowder" is used to indicate any thick and hearty soup with large pieces of food.

CHEESY BROCCOLI SOUP IN A BREAD BOWL

This creamy, cheesy broccoli soup tastes just like Panera Bread's version! My family requests it all the time. You can even serve it in your own homemade bread bowls.
—Rachel Preus, Marshall, MI

PREP: 15 MIN. • **COOK:** 30 MIN. • **MAKES:** 6 SERVINGS

¼ cup butter, cubed
½ cup chopped onion
2 garlic cloves, minced
4 cups fresh broccoli florets (about 8 oz.)
1 large carrot, finely chopped
3 cups chicken stock
2 cups half-and-half cream
2 bay leaves
½ tsp. salt
¼ tsp. ground nutmeg
¼ tsp. pepper
¼ cup cornstarch
¼ cup water or additional chicken stock
2½ cups shredded cheddar cheese
6 small round bread loaves (about 8 oz. each), optional
Optional toppings: Crumbled cooked bacon, additional shredded cheddar cheese, ground nutmeg and pepper

1. In a 6-qt. stockpot, heat butter over medium heat; saute onion and garlic until tender, 6-8 minutes. Stir in broccoli, carrot, stock, cream and seasonings; bring to a boil. Simmer, uncovered, until vegetables are tender, 10-12 minutes.

2. Mix cornstarch and water until smooth; stir into soup. Bring to a boil, stirring occasionally; cook and stir until thickened, 1-2 minutes. Remove bay leaves. Stir in cheese until melted.

3. If using bread bowls, cut a slice off the top of each bread loaf; hollow out bottoms, leaving ¼-in.-thick shells (save removed bread for another use). Fill with soup just before serving.

4. Serve soup with toppings as desired.

1 CUP: 422 cal., 32g fat (19g sat. fat), 107mg chol., 904mg sod., 15g carb. (5g sugars, 2g fiber), 17g pro.

TEST KITCHEN TIP

These make for a hearty meal on their own but are also delicious as a petite first course. Smaller, sturdy breads such as hard rolls are a good choice.

HOW TO SLICE BASIL
To get perfect ribbons
of basil, try a technique
called chiffonading. Roll
up a stack of basil leaves,
with the largest leaves
on the bottom and the
smaller ones on top. Then,
with a sharp knife, slice
crosswise into thin strips.

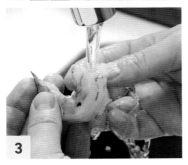

HOW TO PEEL & DEVEIN SHRIMP

Step 1: Start on the underside by head area to remove shell from shrimp. Pull legs and first section of shell to 1 side. Continue pulling shell up and off. Remove tail shell if desired.

Step 2: Remove the black vein running down the back of the shrimp by making a shallow slit with a paring knife along the back from the head area to the tail.

Step 3: Rinse shrimp under cold water to remove all traces of vein.

THAI SHRIMP SOUP

This tasty crowd-pleasing soup comes together in minutes, and I like the fact that the ingredients are available in my little local grocery store.
—Jessie Grearson, Falmouth, ME

PREP: 20 MIN. • **COOK:** 20 MIN. • **MAKES:** 8 SERVINGS (2 QT.)

- 1 medium onion, chopped
- 1 Tbsp. olive oil
- 3 cups reduced-sodium chicken broth
- 1 cup water
- 1 Tbsp. brown sugar
- 1 Tbsp. minced fresh gingerroot
- 1 Tbsp. fish sauce or soy sauce
- 1 Tbsp. red curry paste
- 1 lemongrass stalk
- 1 lb. uncooked large shrimp, peeled and deveined
- 1½ cups frozen shelled edamame
- 1 can (13.66 oz.) light coconut milk
- 1 can (8¾ oz.) whole baby corn, drained and cut in half
- ½ cup bamboo shoots
- ¼ cup fresh basil leaves, julienned
- ¼ cup minced fresh cilantro
- 2 Tbsp. lime juice
- 1½ tsp. grated lime zest
- 1 tsp. curry powder

1. In a Dutch oven, saute onion in oil until tender. Add the broth, water, brown sugar, ginger, fish sauce, curry paste and lemongrass. Bring to a boil. Reduce heat; carefully stir in shrimp and edamame. Cook, uncovered, for 5-6 minutes or until shrimp turn pink.

2. Add the coconut milk, corn, bamboo shoots, basil, cilantro, lime juice, lime zest and curry powder; heat through. Discard lemongrass.

1 CUP: 163 cal., 7g fat (3g sat. fat), 69mg chol., 505mg sod., 9g carb. (5g sugars, 2g fiber), 14g pro. **DIABETIC EXCHANGES:** 2 lean meat, 1 vegetable, 1 fat.

HOMEMADE BONE BROTH

Bone broth is excellent in place of stocks or broths called for in recipes. It's also great on its own or as a base for soup.
—*Taste of Home* Test Kitchen

PREP: 1½ HOURS + COOLING • **COOK:** 8-24 HOURS • **MAKES:** ABOUT 2½ QT.

4 **lbs. meaty beef soup bones (beef shanks or short ribs)**
2 **medium onions, quartered**
3 **chopped medium carrots, optional**
½ **cup warm water (110° to 115°)**
3 **bay leaves**
3 **garlic cloves, peeled**
8 **to 10 whole peppercorns**
 Cold water

1. Place the bones in a stockpot or Dutch oven; add enough water to cover. Bring to a boil over medium-high heat; reduce heat and simmer 15 minutes. Drain, discarding liquid. Rinse bones; drain.

2. Meanwhile, preheat oven to 450°. In a large roasting pan, roast the boiled bones, uncovered, 30 minutes. Add onions and, if desired, carrots. Roast until bones and vegetables are dark brown, 30-45 minutes longer; drain fat.

3. Transfer bones and vegetables to a stockpot or Dutch oven. Add ½ cup warm water to roasting pan; stir to loosen browned bits. Transfer pan juices to pot. Add seasonings and enough cold water just to cover. Slowly bring to a boil; this should take about 30 minutes. Reduce heat; simmer, covered, with lid slightly ajar, 8-24 hours, skimming foam occasionally. If necessary, add water to keep ingredients covered.

4. Remove beef bones; cool. Strain broth through a cheesecloth-lined colander, discarding vegetables and seasonings. If using immediately, skim fat. Or, refrigerate 8 hours or overnight; remove fat from surface.

1 CUP: 30 cal., 0 fat (0 sat. fat), 0 chol., 75mg sod., 0 carb. (0 sugars, 0 fiber), 6g pro.

COLLAGEN-RICH BONE BROTH

Whether you're adding it to soups or sipping it straight, this nutritious stock is well worth the effort. You'll want to simmer it for 8-24 hours to extract lots of collagen and flavor, so we recommend making it a weekend project. Freeze any leftover bone broth for up to 6 months.

GRANDMOTHER'S SOUTHERN CHICKEN AND DUMPLINGS

When I was a child, my grandmother could feed our whole big family with a single chicken—and lots of dumplings.
—Cathy Carroll, Bossier City, LA

PREP: 45 MIN. + STANDING • **COOK:** 30 MIN. • **MAKES:** 10 SERVINGS (2½ QT.)

- 1 **large chicken (6 lbs.)**
- 2 **medium carrots, chopped**
- 2 **celery ribs, sliced**
- 1 **large onion, sliced**
- 4 **qt. water**
- 2 **Tbsp. white vinegar**
- 2 **tsp. salt**

DUMPLINGS
- 2 **cups all-purpose flour**
- 1½ **tsp. salt**
- 1 **large egg**
- ½ **cup reserved chicken broth**
- ½ **tsp. pepper**

1. Place the chicken, carrots, celery and onion in a large Dutch oven or stockpot. Add water, vinegar and salt (adding more water, if necessary, to cover chicken). Bring to a boil. Reduce heat; cover and simmer until meat nearly falls from the bones. Remove chicken from broth; allow to cool. Strain broth, discarding vegetables and seasonings.

2. Remove meat from bones; discard skin and bones. Cut meat into bite-sized pieces; set aside and keep warm. Set aside 1 cup broth; cool to lukewarm.

3. To make dumplings, combine flour and salt. Make a well in flour; add egg. Gradually stir ¼ cup reserved broth into egg, picking up flour as you go. Continue until flour is used up, adding additional broth as needed until dough is consistency of pie dough. Pour any remaining reserved broth back into stockpot.

4. Turn dough onto a floured surface; knead in additional flour to make a stiff dough. Let dough rest for 15 minutes. On a floured surface, roll out dough into a 17-in. square. Cut into 1-in. square pieces. Dust with additional flour; let dry for 30-60 minutes.

5. Bring broth to a boil (you should have about 4 qt.). Drop dumplings into boiling broth. Reduce heat; cover and simmer until a toothpick inserted into center of a dumpling comes out clean (do not lift the cover while simmering), about 10 minutes. Stir in reserved chicken and the pepper.

1 CUP: 310 cal., 9g fat (2g sat. fat), 114mg chol., 981mg sod., 22g carb. (2g sugars, 1g fiber), 34g pro.

MEATLESS MAINS

Whether it's Meatless Monday or a way of life, going meatless means serious benefits to your health and wallet. Here, you'll take on restaurant pad thai, majestic eggplant Parmesan and the ultimate veggie burger.

VEGETABLE PAD THAI

The classic flavors of Thailand abound in this fragrant and flavorful dish. Tofu gives the entree its satisfying protein.

—Sara Landry, Brookline, MA

PREP: 25 MIN. • **COOK:** 15 MIN. • **MAKES:** 6 SERVINGS

- 1 pkg. (12 oz.) whole wheat fettuccine
- ¼ cup rice vinegar
- 3 Tbsp. reduced-sodium soy sauce
- 2 Tbsp. brown sugar
- 2 Tbsp. fish sauce or additional reduced-sodium soy sauce
- 1 Tbsp. lime juice
  Dash Louisiana-style hot sauce
- 3 tsp. canola oil, divided

- 1 pkg. (12 oz.) extra-firm tofu, drained and cut into ½-in. cubes
- 2 medium carrots, grated
- 2 cups fresh snow peas
- 3 garlic cloves, minced
- 2 large eggs, lightly beaten
- 2 cups bean sprouts
- 3 green onions, chopped
- ½ cup minced fresh cilantro
- ¼ cup unsalted peanuts, chopped

1. Cook fettuccine according to package directions. Meanwhile, in a small bowl, combine vinegar, soy sauce, brown sugar, fish sauce, lime juice and hot sauce until smooth; set aside.

2. In a large skillet or wok, heat 2 tsp. oil over medium-high heat. Add tofu; cook and stir until golden brown, 4-6 minutes. Remove and keep warm. Cook and stir the carrots and snow peas in remaining 1 tsp. oil until crisp-tender, 3-5 minutes. Add garlic; cook 1 minute longer. Add eggs; cook and stir until set.

3. Drain pasta; add to the vegetable mixture. Stir vinegar mixture and add to the skillet. Bring to a boil. Add the tofu, bean sprouts and onions; heat through. Sprinkle with cilantro and peanuts.

1⅓ CUPS: 404 cal., 11g fat (2g sat. fat), 62mg chol., 951mg sod., 59g carb. (13g sugars, 9g fiber), 20g pro.

TOFU'S TERRIFIC!

Tofu is a nutritional powerhouse loaded with protein, yet it contains no animal products. Its versatility and affordable price make it ideal for many vegetarian meals.

There are two types of tofu: fresh and silken. Fresh tofu is a firm block that slices easily. It's delicious in soups and stir-fries. It makes Vegetable Pad Thai a satisfying meat- and dairy-free meal. You can find it in the dairy or refrigerated produce section in most stores.

Packed in water and perishable once opened, fresh tofu should be well-drained before using. To drain, wrap tofu in a clean kitchen towel and weigh it down to push out excess moisture (see below).

Silken tofu (on store shelves near the Asian foods) has a smooth, creamy texture. It's perfect for recipes like vegan cheesecakes or smoothies.

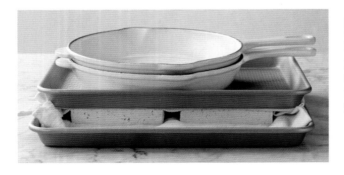

HOW TO DRAIN TOFU

Line a rimmed baking sheet with a clean kitchen towel and place tofu in a single layer on top. Cover tofu with another clean towel and place a second baking sheet on top. Weigh the top pan down with some heavy pans or books. Let the tofu stand for 30 minutes before marinating or cooking.

**BROWSE 50
BEAN-BASED
VEGETARIAN
RECIPES**
Just hover your
camera here.

MEATLESS CHILI MAC

I came across this recipe in a newspaper years ago. It's been a hit at our house ever since. It's fast and flavorful, and it appeals to all ages.
—Cindy Ragan, North Huntingdon, PA

PREP: 15 MIN. • **COOK:** 25 MIN. • **MAKES:** 8 SERVINGS

1 large onion, chopped
1 medium green pepper, chopped
1 Tbsp. olive oil
1 garlic clove, minced
2 cups water
1½ cups uncooked elbow macaroni
1 can (16 oz.) mild chili beans, undrained
1 can (15½ oz.) great northern beans, rinsed and drained
1 can (14½ oz.) diced tomatoes, undrained
1 can (8 oz.) tomato sauce
4 tsp. chili powder
1 tsp. ground cumin
½ tsp. salt
½ cup fat-free sour cream

1. In a Dutch oven, saute onion and green pepper in oil until tender. Add garlic; cook 1 minute longer. Stir in the water, macaroni, beans, tomatoes, tomato sauce, chili powder, cumin and salt.

2. Bring to a boil. Reduce heat; cover and simmer for 15-20 minutes or until macaroni is tender. Top each serving with 1 Tbsp. sour cream.

1¼ CUPS: 206 cal., 3g fat (1g sat. fat), 1mg chol., 651mg sod., 37g carb. (6g sugars, 9g fiber), 10g pro. **DIABETIC EXCHANGES:** 2 starch, 1 vegetable, 1 lean meat.

COOL BEANS

Beans are an easy and affordable way to get the protein and fiber you need each day. The nutritional one-two punch of protein and fiber means you'll stay fuller longer, which can help you eat less.

Beans are a good source of protein, making them an excellent meat alternative for vegetarians. Because beans are so hearty and satisfying, bean-based recipes are also popular with non-vegetarians.

Whether you follow a vegetarian diet or not, try these easy and tasty ways to work beans into your meals:

- Snack on vegetarian refried beans warmed in a tortilla, or try hummus with pita wedges.

- Add beans to the meat or vegetarian meat crumbles in taco or other southwest recipes to thriftily stretch your protein source.

- Sprinkle black beans or chickpeas over a salad or stir beans into soup.

PORTOBELLO & CHICKPEA SHEET-PAN SUPPER

Here's a fantastic meatless dinner or an amazing side dish. It works well with a variety of pan-roasted vegetables. We enjoy using zucchini or squash in the summer. You can also change up the herbs in the dressing.
—Elisabeth Larsen, Pleasant Grove, UT

PREP: 15 MIN. • **BAKE:** 35 MIN. • **MAKES:** 4 SERVINGS

¼ cup olive oil
2 Tbsp. balsamic vinegar
1 Tbsp. minced fresh oregano
¾ tsp. garlic powder
½ tsp. salt
¼ tsp. pepper
1 can (15 oz.) chickpeas or garbanzo beans, rinsed and drained

4 large portobello mushrooms (4 to 4½ in.), stems removed
1 lb. fresh asparagus, trimmed and cut into 2-in. pieces
8 oz. cherry tomatoes

1. Preheat oven to 400°. In a small bowl, combine the first 6 ingredients. Toss chickpeas with 2 Tbsp. oil mixture. Transfer to a 15x10x1-in. baking pan. Bake 20 minutes.

2. Brush mushrooms with 1 Tbsp. oil mixture; add to pan. Toss asparagus and tomatoes with remaining oil mixture; arrange around mushrooms. Bake until vegetables are tender, 15-20 minutes longer.

1 MUSHROOM WITH 1 CUP VEGETABLES: 279 cal., 16g fat (2g sat. fat), 0 chol., 448mg sod., 28g carb. (8g sugars, 7g fiber), 8g pro. **DIABETIC EXCHANGES:** 3 fat, 2 starch.

HOW TO PREP ASPARAGUS

Step 1: To clean, rinse asparagus stalks well in cold water. The tender stalk should easily break from the tough white portion when gently bent. If not, cut off the tough white portion.

Step 2: If stalks are large, use a vegetable peeler to gently peel the tough area of the stalk from the end to just below the tip.

Step 3: If tips are large, scrape off scales with a knife.

PORTOBELLOS SATISFY

Portobellos are large mushrooms with caps several inches in diameter. They are tasty marinated, grilled and served on buns as vegetarian burgers. They also work as a stand-in for meat in casseroles and other dishes.

They are fully grown cremini mushrooms, cousins of the familiar button mushrooms available in most stores. Use creminis (sometimes labeled as baby portobellos) instead of button mushrooms any time you'd like an easy flavor boost.

The portobellos' stems are tough and woody; either discard them or use coarsely chopped and well-rinsed stems in soups or broth.

With their rich taste and meaty texture, portobello mushrooms make any vegetarian meal feel wonderfully satisfying.

**SEE US
MAKE IT**
Just hover your
camera here.

THE BEST EVER
GRILLED CHEESE
SANDWICH

HAM & APPLE

FRESH
BERRIES

BACON &
AVOCADO

THE BEST EVER GRILLED CHEESE SANDWICH

Ooey, gooey and grilled to perfection, this is the ultimate grilled cheese sandwich. Flavorful ingredient upgrades make this grown-up take on the familiar favorite feel like an indulgence.
—Josh Rink, Milwaukee, WI

TAKES: 25 MIN. • **MAKES:** 4 SERVINGS

6 Tbsp. butter, softened, divided
8 slices sourdough bread
3 Tbsp. mayonnaise
3 Tbsp. finely shredded Manchego or Parmesan cheese
⅛ tsp. onion powder
½ cup shredded sharp white cheddar cheese
½ cup shredded Monterey Jack cheese
½ cup shredded Gruyere cheese
4 oz. Brie cheese, rind removed and sliced

1. Spread 3 Tbsp. butter on 1 side of bread slices. Toast bread, butter side down, in a large skillet or electric griddle over medium-low heat until golden brown, 2-3 minutes; remove. In a small bowl, mix together the mayonnaise, Manchego cheese, onion powder and remaining 3 Tbsp. butter. In another bowl, combine cheddar, Monterey Jack and Gruyere.

2. To assemble sandwiches, top toasted side of 4 bread slices with sliced Brie. Sprinkle the cheddar cheese mixture evenly over Brie. Top with the remaining bread slices, toasted side facing inward. Spread mayonnaise mixture on the outsides of each sandwich. Place in same skillet, and cook until bread is golden brown and cheese is melted, 5-6 minutes on each side. Serve immediately.

1 SANDWICH: 659 cal., 49g fat (27g sat. fat), 122mg chol., 1017mg sod., 30g carb. (3g sugars, 1g fiber), 24g pro.

MAKE IT YOUR OWN

• **Ham & Apple:** After sprinkling with the cheddar cheese mixture, top with thinly sliced ham and apple slices. Proceed as directed.

• **Fresh Berries:** Scatter fresh blackberries and raspberries on top of the cheddar cheese mixture inside the sandwich. Proceed as directed.

• **Bacon & Avocado:** Layer crisp bacon slices on top of the cheddar cheese mixture. Top with sliced tomato and avocado and remaining bread slices. Proceed as directed.

THE SECRET BEHIND THE WORLD'S BEST GRILLED CHEESE

The Best Bread: Sourdough
A good crusty bread like sourdough will stand up to all the gooeyness going on inside the sandwich. And its robust flavor won't get lost when paired with the rich cheeses.

The Right Spread: Mayo Mixture
A mixture of mayo and butter spread on the bread creates a delightfully crispy crust that doesn't skimp on the well-loved buttery flavor one expects on a grilled cheese.

The Ideal Cheeses: Flavorful and Melty

• **Manchego** has a low moisture content that makes for those lovely crispy bits on the outer edge of the sandwich.

• **Sharp White Cheddar** provides the perfect amount of tangy flavor.

• **Monterey Jack** adds an irresistibly gooey effect when the sandwich is sliced and pulled apart.

• **Gruyere** gives the sandwich a nutty boost of flavor.

• **Brie** has a creamy texture that makes it melty and slightly sophisticated.

BAKED FETA PASTA

There's a reason this recipe went viral on TikTok! Baked Feta Pasta is about to become a new household favorite. It's simple to throw together and incredibly creamy and delicious.
—Alicia Rooker, Milwaukee, WI

PREP: 15 MIN. • **BAKE:** 30 MIN. • **MAKES:** 8 SERVINGS

2   **pints cherry tomatoes**
3   **garlic cloves, halved**
½   **cup olive oil**
1   **pkg. (8 oz.) block feta cheese**
1   **tsp. sea salt**
¼   **tsp. coarsely ground pepper**
1   **pkg. (16 oz.) rigatoni or other short pasta**
    Fresh basil leaves, coarsely chopped

1. Preheat oven to 400°. In a 13x9-in. baking dish, combine tomatoes, garlic and ¼ cup olive oil. Place the block of feta in the center, moving tomatoes so cheese is sitting on the pan bottom. Drizzle feta with the remaining oil and sprinkle with salt and pepper. Bake until tomato skins start to split and the garlic has softened, 30-40 minutes.

2. Meanwhile, cook pasta according to package directions for al dente. Drain, reserving 1 cup pasta water.

3. Stir feta mixture, lightly pressing tomatoes, until combined. Add pasta and toss to combine. Stir in enough reserved pasta water to achieve the desired consistency. Sprinkle with basil.

1 SERVING: 373 cal., 16g fat (6g sat. fat), 25mg chol., 507mg sod., 46g carb. (5g sugars, 3g fiber), 12g pro.

HOW TO QUICKLY SEPARATE AND PEEL GARLIC CLOVES

Step 1: Place the head of garlic in a bowl and smash with the bottom of a similar-sized bowl. You can also smash between 2 cutting boards.

Step 2: Put the whole crushed bulb in a hard-sided bowl with a similar-sized bowl over the top. Metal is best, but you can use glass or even a firm plastic food storage container with a lid. A jar works, too, but it takes longer to shake.

Step 3: Shake the bowls vigorously for 10-15 seconds to separate the papery outer layer from the garlic clove.

Step 4: The cloves are peeled and the skin can be easily discarded.

PAN WITH A PLAN

This crowd-sized pasta dish is picture-perfect from start to finish. First, roast feta, tomatoes, garlic and oil. Then stir in cooked pasta and serve!

BEST EVER VEGGIE BURGER

I was on the hunt for a veggie burger that tasted good, didn't fall apart on the grill and was easy to make. So I decided to create my own recipe.
—Sarah Tramonte, Milwaukee, WI

PREP: 30 MIN. • **COOK:** 10 MIN. • **MAKES:** 4 SERVINGS

1 cup canned black beans, rinsed and drained
1 cup chopped walnuts
1½ tsp. ground cumin
½ tsp. ground fennel seed
¼ tsp. smoked paprika
1 Tbsp. oil from sun-dried tomatoes
¼ cup shredded carrot
1 large shallot, minced
2 Tbsp. oil-packed sun-dried tomatoes, chopped

1 garlic clove, minced
¼ cup old-fashioned oats
1 Tbsp. chia seeds
2 tsp. reduced-sodium soy sauce
½ tsp. garlic salt
1 Tbsp. olive oil
Optional: Barbecue sauce, toasted hamburger buns, Sriracha mayo, lettuce, red onion and tomato

1. Preheat oven to 325°. Spread beans evenly on a parchment-lined rimmed baking pan. Bake until beans start to split open, 6-8 minutes.

2. Meanwhile, in a large dry nonstick skillet over medium heat, cook and stir walnuts, cumin, fennel and smoked paprika 2-3 minutes or until fragrant. Remove from pan and cool. In the same skillet, heat oil from sun-dried tomatoes over medium heat. Add carrot, shallot and sun-dried tomatoes; cook and stir until tender, about 5 minutes. Add the garlic; cook 1 minute longer. Remove from the heat; cool slightly.

3. Transfer carrot mixture to a food processor. Add the beans, walnut mixture, oats, chia seeds, soy sauce and garlic salt. Pulse until combined. Shape into four 4-in. patties.

4. In the same skillet over medium heat, cook the patties in olive oil until browned, 3-4 minutes on each side. If desired, baste with barbecue sauce and serve on buns with toppings of your choice.

1 BURGER: 357 cal., 28g fat (3g sat. fat), 0 chol., 479mg sod., 22g carb. (2g sugars, 7g fiber), 9g pro.

TASTY LENTIL TACOS

My husband has to watch his cholesterol. Finding dishes that are healthy for him and yummy for our five children is a challenge sometimes, but this meatless take on tacos is a huge hit with everyone.
—Michelle Thomas, Bangor, ME

PREP: 15 MIN. • **COOK:** 40 MIN. • **MAKES:** 6 SERVINGS

1 tsp. canola oil
1 medium onion, finely chopped
1 garlic clove, minced
1 cup dried lentils, rinsed
1 Tbsp. chili powder
2 tsp. ground cumin
1 tsp. dried oregano
2½ cups vegetable broth

1 cup salsa
12 taco shells
1½ cups shredded lettuce
1 cup chopped fresh tomatoes
1½ cups shredded reduced-fat cheddar cheese
6 Tbsp. fat-free sour cream

1. In a large nonstick skillet, heat oil over medium heat; saute onion and garlic until tender. Add lentils and seasonings; cook and stir 1 minute. Stir in broth; bring to a boil. Reduce heat; simmer, covered, until lentils are tender, 25-30 minutes.

2. Cook, uncovered, until the mixture is thickened, 6-8 minutes, stirring occasionally. Mash lentils slightly; stir in salsa and heat through. Serve in taco shells. Top with remaining ingredients.

2 TACOS: 365 cal., 12g fat (5g sat. fat), 21mg chol., 777mg sod., 44g carb. (5g sugars, 6g fiber), 19g pro. **DIABETIC EXCHANGES:** 2½ starch, 2 lean meat, 1 vegetable, 1 fat.

LEAN, GREEN, MIGHTY LENTILS

Ounce for ounce, lentils have as much protein as steak (with less than 10% of the fat!) A half-cup of these pulses (a type of legume, like dried peas or chickpeas) provides you with 9 grams of protein and 8 grams of healthy fiber—that's almost a third of the daily recommended amount! A diet rich in lentils and other pulses can reduce your risk of cancer, diabetes and heart disease.

Lentils use few resources to grow and, calorie for calorie, produce only 2.5% as much of the greenhouse gas carbon dioxide as beef and 10% as much carbon dioxide as tofu. That makes lentils one of the greenest crops there is—especially when you factor in their high protein and fiber content.

Billions of people around the world rely on lentils and legumes as protein in their diets. These satisfying, economical plants are a major food source throughout the Americas, Caribbean, Mediterranean and parts of Asia.

SALTING EGGPLANTS

Salting eggplant is an optional step for larger fruits that may taste bitter. To salt, place slices, cubes or strips of eggplant in a colander over a plate; sprinkle eggplant with salt and toss. Let stand for 30 minutes. Rinse, drain well and pat dry with paper towels.

THE BEST EGGPLANT PARMESAN

I love eggplant and have many recipes that include it, but this one is my favorite. The cheeses and seasonings make this dish unforgettable.
—Dorothy Kilpatrick, Wilmington, NC

PREP: 1¼ HOURS • **BAKE:** 35 MIN. + STANDING
MAKES: 2 CASSEROLES (8 SERVINGS EACH)

- 3 garlic cloves, minced
- ⅓ cup olive oil
- 2 cans (28 oz. each) crushed tomatoes
- 1 cup pitted ripe olives, chopped
- ¼ cup thinly sliced fresh basil leaves or 1 Tbsp. dried basil
- 3 Tbsp. capers, drained
- 1 tsp. crushed red pepper flakes
- ¼ tsp. pepper

EGGPLANT

- 1 cup all-purpose flour
- 4 large eggs, beaten
- 3 cups dry bread crumbs
- 1 Tbsp. garlic powder

- 1 Tbsp. minced fresh oregano or 1 tsp. dried oregano
- 4 small eggplants (about 1 lb. each), peeled and cut lengthwise into ½-in. slices
- 1 cup olive oil

CHEESE

- 2 large eggs, beaten
- 2 cartons (15 oz. each) ricotta cheese
- 1¼ cups shredded Parmesan cheese, divided
- ½ cup thinly sliced fresh basil leaves or 2 Tbsp. dried basil
- ½ tsp. pepper
- 8 cups shredded part-skim mozzarella cheese

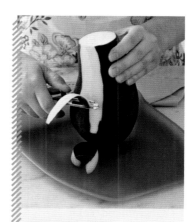

HOW TO PEEL AN EGGPLANT

Cut the stem end off the eggplant, and, if desired, a small slice from the bottom so the eggplant can rest flat. Remove the skin with a vegetable peeler. Eggplant peel can be tough and bitter and is best removed in most recipes. However, some small varieties of eggplant are completely edible, including the peel.

1. In a Dutch oven over medium heat, cook garlic in oil 1 minute. Stir in tomatoes, olives, basil, capers, pepper flakes and pepper. Bring to a boil. Reduce heat; simmer, uncovered, 45-60 minutes or until thickened.

2. Meanwhile, for eggplant, place flour and eggs in separate shallow bowls. In another bowl, combine bread crumbs, garlic powder and oregano. Dip eggplant in flour, eggs, then bread crumb mixture.

3. In a large skillet, cook eggplant in batches in oil for 5 minutes on each side or until tender. Drain on paper towels. In a large bowl, combine the eggs, ricotta, ½ cup Parmesan cheese, basil and pepper.

4. Preheat oven to 350°. In each of 2 greased 13x9-in. baking dishes, layer 1½ cups tomato sauce, 4 eggplant slices, 1 cup ricotta mixture and 2 cups mozzarella cheese. Repeat the layers. Sprinkle each with the remaining Parmesan cheese. Bake, uncovered, 35-40 minutes or until bubbly. Let stand for 10 minutes before cutting. If desired, sprinkle with additional fresh basil.

1 PIECE: 585 cal., 40g fat (14g sat. fat), 132mg chol., 935mg sod., 32g carb. (11g sugars, 7g fiber), 29g pro.

VEGAN BUTTER CAULIFLOWER

I created this Indian butter cauliflower recipe for all the foodies in my family who love ethnic food. It gets high marks from vegans and non-vegans alike.
—Mihaela Metaxa-Albu, London, NY

PREP: 25 MIN. • **COOK:** 20 MIN. • **MAKES:** 4 SERVINGS

1 large head cauliflower, cut into florets
2 Tbsp. coconut oil, melted
1 Tbsp. minced fresh gingerroot
2 garlic cloves, minced
1 tsp. garam masala
¼ tsp. salt
¼ tsp. pepper

SAUCE
1 Tbsp. olive oil
½ cup chopped onion
1 Tbsp. minced fresh gingerroot
2 garlic cloves, minced
2 tsp. garam masala
2 tsp. curry powder
1 tsp. cayenne pepper, optional
1 can (15 oz.) crushed tomatoes
1 can (13.66 oz.) coconut milk
¼ tsp. salt
¼ tsp. pepper
¼ cup chopped fresh cilantro
Optional: Hot cooked rice, naan flatbreads and lime wedges

1. Preheat broiler. In a large bowl, combine first 7 ingredients; toss to coat. Transfer to a rimmed baking sheet. Broil 3-4 in. from heat until brown and crisp-tender, 12-15 minutes, turning once.

2. Meanwhile, in a large skillet, heat olive oil over medium-high heat. Add onion; cook and stir until tender, 4-5 minutes. Add ginger, garlic, garam masala, curry powder and, if desired, cayenne pepper; cook 1 minute longer. Stir in the tomatoes, coconut milk, salt and pepper. Bring to a boil; reduce the heat. Simmer, uncovered, until thickened, 10-12 minutes, stirring occasionally. Stir in cauliflower; sprinkle with cilantro. If desired, serve with rice, naan and lime wedges.

1½ CUPS: 349 cal., 27g fat (22g sat. fat), 0 chol., 584mg sod., 24g carb. (11g sugars, 7g fiber), 8g pro.

AIR-FRIED VARIATION

Preheat the air fryer to 400°. Working in batches if necessary, place cauliflower in a single layer on greased tray in air-fryer basket. Cook until brown and crisp-tender, 8-10 minutes, turning once.

Meanwhile, prepare sauce as recipe directs. Stir in cauliflower; sprinkle with cilantro.

LEARN TO
MAKE NAAN
Just hover your
camera here.

SEAFOOD

No need to fear: Choosing and preparing seafood dinners is a snap with the go-to recipes and pointers in this chapter. Plus, you'll discover inspiration throughout to get creative and make each dish your own.

TILAPIA FLORENTINE

Get a little more heart-healthy fish into your weekly diet with this quick and easy entree. Topped with fresh spinach and a splash of lemon, it's sure to become a favorite!
—Melanie Bachman, Ulysses, PA

TAKES: 30 MIN. • **MAKES:** 4 SERVINGS

1   pkg. (6 oz.) fresh baby spinach
6   tsp. canola oil, divided
4   tilapia fillets (4 oz. each)
2   Tbsp. lemon juice
2   tsp. garlic-herb seasoning blend
1   large egg, room temperature, lightly beaten
½   cup part-skim ricotta cheese
¼   cup grated Parmesan cheese
    Lemon wedges, optional

1. Preheat oven to 375°. In a large nonstick skillet, cook spinach in 4 tsp. oil until wilted; drain. Meanwhile, place tilapia in a greased 13x9-in. baking dish. Drizzle with lemon juice and remaining 2 tsp. oil. Sprinkle with seasoning blend.

2. In a small bowl, combine the egg, ricotta cheese and spinach; spoon over fillets. Sprinkle with Parmesan cheese.

3. Bake until fish just begins to flake easily with a fork, 15-20 minutes. If desired, serve with lemon wedges and additional Parmesan cheese.

1 SERVING: 249 cal., 13g fat (4g sat. fat), 122mg chol., 307mg sod., 4g carb. (1g sugars, 1g fiber), 29g pro.

TILAPIA FLORENTINE TIPS

Can you use other types of fish instead of tilapia? Yes, you can use other types of fish—any lean whitefish will work, including cod, sole, swai or snapper.

Can you use frozen spinach instead of fresh spinach? Frozen spinach can be used in place of fresh. Just make sure you thaw the spinach and drain most of the liquid before proceeding with the recipe.

What's the best way to reheat leftovers? Reheating in your microwave is probably your best bet to prevent your tilapia from drying out. Placing a damp towel or microwave-safe lid over fish when reheating can help prevent dryness.

DEFROSTING FISH

- **In the Refrigerator:** Place a tray under the package to catch any liquid or juices. Allow 12 or more hours for a 1-lb. package.

- **In Cold Water:** Place fish or shellfish in a leakproof bag or container. Submerge container in cold tap water. Change the water every 30 minutes. Allow 1-2 hours per pound.

**WATCH THE
2-MINUTE
HOW-TO**
Just hover your
camera here.

SEAFOOD LASAGNA

This rich, satisfying dish is loaded with scallops, shrimp and imitation crab in a creamy sauce. I consider it the crown jewel in my repertoire of recipes.
—Elena Hansen, Ruidoso, NM

PREP: 35 MIN. • **BAKE:** 35 MIN. + STANDING • **MAKES:** 12 SERVINGS

- 1 green onion, finely chopped
- 2 Tbsp. canola oil
- 2 Tbsp. plus ½ cup butter, divided
- ½ cup chicken broth
- 1 bottle (8 oz.) clam juice
- 1 lb. bay scallops
- 1 lb. uncooked small shrimp, peeled and deveined
- 1 pkg. (8 oz.) imitation crabmeat, chopped
- ¼ tsp. white pepper, divided
- ½ cup all-purpose flour
- 1½ cups 2% milk
- ½ tsp. salt
- 1 cup heavy whipping cream
- ½ cup shredded Parmesan cheese, divided
- 9 lasagna noodles, cooked and drained

1. In a large skillet, saute onion in oil and 2 Tbsp. butter until tender. Stir in broth and clam juice; bring to a boil. Add the scallops, shrimp, imitation crab and ⅛ tsp. pepper; return to a boil. Reduce heat; simmer, uncovered, for 4-5 minutes or until the shrimp turn pink and scallops are firm and opaque, stirring gently. Drain, reserving cooking liquid; set seafood mixture aside.

2. In a large saucepan, melt the remaining butter; stir in flour until smooth. Combine milk and reserved cooking liquid; gradually add to the saucepan. Add salt and remaining pepper. Bring to a boil; cook and stir for 2 minutes or until thickened.

3. Remove from the heat; stir in cream and ¼ cup cheese. Stir ¾ cup white sauce into the seafood mixture.

4. Preheat oven to 350°. Spread ½ cup white sauce in a greased 13x9-in. baking dish. Top with 3 noodles; spread with half of the seafood mixture and 1¼ cups sauce. Repeat layers. Top with remaining noodles, sauce and cheese.

5. Bake, uncovered, for 35-40 minutes or until golden brown. Let stand for 15 minutes before cutting.

1 PIECE: 386 cal., 22g fat (12g sat. fat), 111mg chol., 633mg sod., 28g carb. (3g sugars, 1g fiber), 19g pro.

HOW TO FREEZE LASAGNA

Step 1: Assemble your favorite lasagna recipe, then let it cool completely.

Step 2: Cover lasagna tightly with plastic wrap and foil. This will keep air from reaching the lasagna, preventing freezer burn and preserving its flavor and texture. First wrap the entire lasagna, pan included, in plastic wrap. Try to get the plastic wrap as close to the lasagna's surface as you can to block out air. Next, cover the top of the wrapped lasagna with foil.

Step 3: Label and freeze. Write the recipe name, best-by date (up to 3 months in the future) and reheating instructions on masking tape, then place tape on the foil. You can also write directly on the foil, but be careful not to puncture it.

Step 4: Thaw lasagna in the refrigerator 1-2 nights. Unwrap; let stand at room temperature 30 minutes. Cover with foil and bake.

CITRUS SALMON EN PAPILLOTE

This salmon dish is so simple and easy to make—
yet so delicious, elegant and impressive.
—Dahlia Abrams, Detroit, MI

PREP: 20 MIN. • **BAKE:** 15 MIN. • **MAKES:** 6 SERVINGS

6 orange slices	½ tsp. salt
6 lime slices	¼ tsp. pepper
6 salmon fillets (4 oz. each)	2 Tbsp. minced fresh parsley
1 lb. fresh asparagus, trimmed and halved	3 Tbsp. lemon juice
Olive oil-flavored cooking spray	

1. Preheat oven to 425°. Cut parchment or heavy-duty foil into six 15x10-in. pieces; fold them in half. Arrange citrus slices on 1 side of each piece. Top with fish and asparagus. Spritz with cooking spray. Sprinkle with salt, pepper and parsley. Drizzle with lemon juice.

2. Fold parchment over fish; draw edges together and crimp with fingers to form tightly sealed packets. Place in baking pans.

3. Bake until fish flakes easily with a fork, 12-15 minutes. Open packets carefully to allow steam to escape.

1 PACKET: 224 cal., 13g fat (2g sat. fat), 57mg chol., 261mg sod., 6g carb. (3g sugars, 1g fiber), 20g pro. **DIABETIC EXCHANGES:** 3 lean meat, 1 vegetable.

EN PAPILLOTE COOKING TIPS

Cooking en papillote (a French term for cooking in a paper wrapping) is an easy, healthy way that uses parchment packets to preserve moisture and vitamins. This method uses little to no fat and makes a pretty presentation with zero cleanup. The paper holds in moisture to steam the food, infusing it with flavor from citrus, herbs or other seasonings. En papillote is usually used with fish, but poultry cutlets and all-veggie packets work too.

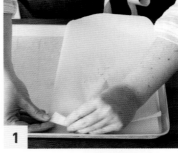

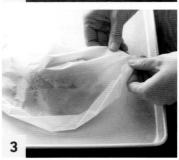

HOW TO FOLD A PARCHMENT PACKET

Step 1: Place parchment on a baking pan, then place food on half of the sheet. Fold paper in half, covering the food.

Step 2: Beginning at a top corner, crimp the edge. Fold paper up and over itself in small sections, letting each fold reinforce the previous one.

Step 3: Continue folding. When you reach the end, fold the edges under: This will help keep the packet from coming undone as steam builds up inside.

FISH & CHIPS

"Tuck in" as though you're in a traditional British pub. These baked fish fillets have a fuss-free coating that's healthy, but just as crunchy and golden as the deep-fried kind. Simply seasoned and also baked, the crispy fries are perfect on the side.
—Janice Mitchell, Aurora, CO

PREP: 10 MIN. • **BAKE:** 35 MIN. • **MAKES:** 4 SERVINGS

1 lb. potatoes (about 2 medium)
2 Tbsp. olive oil
¼ tsp. pepper

FISH
⅓ cup all-purpose flour
¼ tsp. pepper
1 large egg
2 Tbsp. water
⅔ cup crushed cornflakes
1 Tbsp. grated Parmesan cheese
⅛ tsp. cayenne pepper
1 lb. haddock or cod fillets
Tartar sauce, optional

1. Preheat oven to 425°. Peel and cut potatoes lengthwise into ½-in.-thick slices; cut slices into ½-in.-thick sticks.

2. In a large bowl, toss potatoes with oil and pepper. Transfer to a 15x10x1-in. baking pan coated with cooking spray. Bake, uncovered, 25-30 minutes or until golden brown and crisp, stirring once.

3. Meanwhile, in a shallow bowl, mix flour and pepper. In another shallow bowl, whisk egg with water. In a third bowl, toss cornflakes with cheese and cayenne. Dip fish in flour mixture to coat both sides; shake off excess. Dip in the egg mixture, then in the cornflake mixture, patting to help the coating adhere.

4. Place on a baking sheet coated with cooking spray. Bake 10-12 minutes or until the fish just begins to flake easily with a fork. Serve with potatoes and, if desired, tartar sauce.

1 SERVING: 376 cal., 9g fat (2g sat. fat), 120mg chol., 228mg sod., 44g carb. (3g sugars, 2g fiber), 28g pro. **DIABETIC EXCHANGES:** 3 starch, 3 lean meat, 1½ fat.

AIR-FRIED VARIATION

Preheat air fryer to 400°. In batches, place potatoes in a single layer on a greased tray in air-fryer basket; cook until just tender, 5-10 minutes. Toss the potatoes to redistribute; cook until lightly browned and crisp, 5-10 minutes longer.

Meanwhile, season and coat fish.

Remove fries from basket; keep warm. Place fish in a single layer on a greased tray in air-fryer basket. Cook until fish is lightly browned and just beginning to flake easily with a fork, 8-10 minutes, turning once halfway through cooking. Do not overcook. Return fries to basket to heat through if necessary.

CREAMY SCALLOP CREPES

These savory crepes feel so elegant for the holidays. I sometimes like to add a bit of fresh dill weed to the crepe batter before refrigerating.
—Doreen Kelly, Roslyn, PA

PREP: 45 MIN. + CHILLING • **BAKE:** 15 MIN. • **MAKES:** 6 SERVINGS

2 **large egg whites**	⅛ **tsp. white pepper**
1 **large egg**	1 **lb. sliced fresh mushrooms**
1½ **cups fat-free milk**	4 **green onions, sliced**
1 **cup all-purpose flour**	2 **Tbsp. butter**
½ **tsp. salt**	¼ **cup all-purpose flour**
2 **Tbsp. unsalted butter, melted**	⅔ **cup fat-free evaporated milk**
	½ **cup shredded reduced-fat Swiss cheese**
FILLING	**Sliced green onions, optional**
1 **lb. bay scallops**	
½ **cup white wine or reduced-sodium chicken broth**	

1. In a small bowl, beat the egg whites, egg and milk. Combine flour and salt; add to milk mixture and mix well. Cover and refrigerate for 1 hour.

2. Brush an 8-in. nonstick skillet lightly with melted butter; heat. Stir crepe batter; pour 2 Tbsp. into center of skillet. Lift and tilt pan to coat bottom evenly. Cook until top appears dry; turn and cook 15-20 seconds longer. Remove to a wire rack. Repeat with remaining batter, brushing skillet with melted butter as needed. When cool, stack crepes with waxed paper or paper towels in between.

3. In a large nonstick skillet, bring the scallops, wine and pepper to a boil. Reduce heat; simmer until scallops are firm and opaque, 3-4 minutes. Drain, reserving cooking liquid; set liquid and scallops aside.

4. In the same skillet, saute mushrooms and onions in butter until almost tender. Sprinkle with flour; stir until blended. Gradually stir in evaporated milk and cooking liquid. Bring to a boil; cook and stir until thickened, about 2 minutes. Remove from the heat. Stir in cheese and scallops.

5. Spread ⅓ cup filling down the center of each crepe; roll up and place in a 13x9-in. baking dish coated with cooking spray. Cover and bake at 350° until heated through, 12-15 minutes. If desired, sprinkle crepes with sliced green onions.

2 CREPES: 331 cal., 10g fat (6g sat. fat), 76mg chol., 641mg sod., 33g carb. (9g sugars, 2g fiber), 24g pro. **DIABETIC EXCHANGES:** 3 lean meat, 2 starch, 2 fat.

MAKE THEM YOUR OWN WITH SMART, EASY SUBSTITUTIONS

One of the pleasures of cooking is improvising with what you have on hand. Save money and time when making these tasty crepes with simple substitutions:

- Use 2 whole eggs in the crepe batter instead of 2 whites and 1 egg. You will save 1 egg and won't have extra yolks hanging around.

- Substitute medium shrimp for some or all of the scallops.

- If you don't have wine or broth for the filling, substitute ½ tsp. chicken bouillon granules and ½ cup water. Voila! No open or partial cans or bottles.

- Evaporated milk adds a rich creaminess without adding fat. You could substitute ⅔ cup heavy cream or half-and-half, but you'd be increasing the fat. Another option: Lightly simmer 1⅓ cups of low- or no-fat milk in a small heavy saucepan until it is reduced by half. Whisk occasionally.

CREPE SUCCESS TIPS

1) Use a brand-name flour. Some store brands may not blend as seamlessly into the batter as others, which can result in unsightly white lumps. If in doubt, sift your flour or run it through a sieve before using.

2) Rest the batter. This lets every bit of flour fully absorb the liquid, ensuring you'll have no lumps. It also relaxes the gluten, which creates a tender finished crepe.

3) Use quick, efficient movements. Stir the batter after it rests in the fridge, but be mindful not to stir or overwork it after that. Crepes cook fast, so be ready to flip them with a thin, flexible spatula. You can use your fingers to support the flip.

4) Give yourself time. The first crepe is rarely perfect, but crepes get better (and easier to make) after the first 2 or 3. By then, you'll have a perfectly buttered skillet (not too much or too little), and you'll figure out the best temperature for working at a steady rhythm.

CHOOSING LOBSTER TAILS

Cold-water lobsters—from New England, Australia or New Zealand—are more meaty and whiter-fleshed than warm-water (aka spiny) lobsters. They also tend to be more expensive. Spiny lobsters come from the Carolinas, Georgia, Florida and the Caribbean. Though spiny lobsters don't have big claws like the cold-water type, their tail meat is sweeter and more delicate-tasting.

BROILED LOBSTER TAIL

No matter where you live, these succulent, buttery lobster tails are just a few minutes away. Here in Iowa, we use frozen lobster with delicious results, but if you're near the ocean, by all means use fresh!
—Lauren McAnelly, Des Moines, IA

PREP: 30 MIN. • **COOK:** 5 MIN. • **MAKES:** 4 SERVINGS

4 **lobster tails (5 to 6 oz. each), thawed**	**Salt and pepper to taste**
¼ **cup cold butter, cut into thin slices**	**Lemon wedges**

1. Preheat broiler. Using kitchen scissors, cut a 2-in.-wide rectangle from the top shell of each lobster tail; loosen from lobster meat and remove.

2. Pull away edges of remaining shell to release lobster meat from sides; pry meat loose from bottom shell, keeping tail end attached. Place in a foil-lined 15x10x1-in. pan. Arrange butter slices over lobster meat.

3. Broil 5-6 in. from heat until meat is opaque, 5-8 minutes. Season with salt and pepper to taste; serve with lemon wedges.

1 LOBSTER TAIL: 211 cal., 13g fat (8g sat. fat), 211mg chol., 691mg sod., 0 carb. (0 sugars, 0 fiber), 24g pro.

ELEVATE IT WITH A FANCY BUTTER

Nothing goes better with lobster than rich butter!

- **Classic Clarified Butter:** In a heavy saucepan, melt 1 cup butter over low heat. Cook until solids separate from fat, about 10 minutes, but do not let butter brown. Remove from heat; skim and discard surface foam. Slowly pour clear yellow liquid through a fine sieve into a bowl. Serve warm for dipping lobster.

- **Lemon-Chive Compound Butter:** Combine ¼ cup softened butter, 2 Tbsp. chopped fresh chives, 2 Tbsp. chopped fresh parsley, 1 Tbsp. minced shallot, 1 minced garlic clove, ½ tsp. grated lemon peel and ¼ tsp. Transfer mixture to a sheet of waxed paper; roll into a log, then refrigerate until firm. Unwrap, slice and place on lobster tails before broiling.

- **Chimichurri Compound Butter:** Combine ¼ cup softened butter, 2 Tbsp. chopped fresh cilantro, 2 Tbsp. chopped fresh parsley, 1 Tbsp. minced shallot, 1 tsp. grated lemon peel, 1 tsp. minced fresh oregano, 1 minced garlic clove, ¼ tsp. salt and, if desired, ⅛ tsp. crushed red pepper flakes. Unwrap, slice and place on lobster tails before broiling.

COCONUT CITRUS STEAMED COD

I love to make this fusion meal on weeknights when I am short on time but want something big in flavor.
—Roxanne Chan, Albany, CA

TAKES: 30 MIN. • **MAKES:** 4 SERVINGS

4 cod fillets (6 oz. each)	1 can (11 oz.) mandarin oranges, drained
1 Tbsp. cornstarch	1 green onion, chopped
1 cup canned coconut milk	2 Tbsp. sliced almonds
½ cup orange juice	1 Tbsp. sesame oil
2 Tbsp. sweet chili sauce	Minced fresh cilantro
1 tsp. minced fresh gingerroot	
1 tsp. soy sauce	

1. In a large saucepan, place a steamer basket over 1 in. water. Place cod in basket. Bring water to a boil. Reduce heat to maintain a low boil; steam, covered, until fish just begins to flake easily with a fork, 8-10 minutes.

2. Meanwhile, in a small saucepan, whisk cornstarch, coconut milk and orange juice until smooth. Add chili sauce, ginger and soy sauce. Cook and stir over medium heat until thickened, 1-2 minutes. Stir in oranges, green onion, almonds and sesame oil; heat through. Serve with cod; sprinkle with cilantro.

1 SERVING: 330 cal., 15g fat (10g sat. fat), 65mg chol., 316mg sod., 19g carb. (15g sugars, 1g fiber), 29g pro.

HOW TO TEST FISH FOR DONENESS
Ensure perfectly cooked fish with these pointers.

- For fish fillets, insert a fork at an angle into the thickest portion of the fish and gently part the meat. When it is opaque and flakes into sections, it is cooked completely. If it is still translucent, it is undercooked.

- For whole fish, insert a fork along the backbone and the top fillet. The fish is done when the fillet is easily lifted from the bones.

- The USDA recommends an internal temperature of 145°. A good rule of thumb is to cook fish for 10 minutes per inch of thickness (measured at the thickest area). Check the fish's doneness about 2 minutes before the recommended cooking time to avoid overcooking.

HOW TO KEEP FISH FRESH

Fish stays freshest when stored on ice. To keep it ice cold without mess or damaging the fish's texture, place frozen gel packs or blue ice blocks in a container; top with the wrapped fish. Place in the meat drawer and use within a few days. Wash ice packs with hot, soapy water before reusing.

BROWSE 23 CANNED COCONUT MILK RECIPES
Just hover your camera here.

SALMON SAVVY

For the best-tasting salmon, try to shop at a local fishmonger. Specialized fish markets often have a more knowledgeable staff and fresher fish (due to higher turnover). Here's what to check for, no matter where you're buying:

Look at It. Avoid any fish that is discolored or has bruised skin.

Smell It. A fresh fish won't have an offensive "fishy" smell. If a fish smells sour or ammonia-like, it's old and should be avoided.

Press It. Be sure it feels firm, with no gaps where the flesh is pulling apart.

Read the Labels. Fish labeled Atlantic salmon or Norwegian salmon is farm-raised. If you're looking for wild-caught salmon, opt for sockeye, coho or chinook. While farmed and wild salmon are both healthy choices, you may find that you have a taste preference. So it's good to know what the labels mean.

OVEN-ROASTED SALMON

When I'm starving after work, I want a fast meal with a no-fail technique. Roasted salmon is super tender and has a delicate sweetness. It's also an easy wowza for company.
—Jeanne Ambrose, Milwaukee, WI

TAKES: 20 MIN. • **MAKES:** 4 SERVINGS

1 **center-cut salmon fillet** (1½ lbs.)	½ tsp. salt
1 **Tbsp. olive oil**	¼ tsp. pepper

1. Place a large cast-iron or other ovenproof skillet in a cold oven. Preheat the oven to 450°. Meanwhile, brush salmon with oil and sprinkle with salt and pepper.

2. Carefully remove skillet from oven. Place fish, skin side down, in the skillet. Return to oven; bake, uncovered, until salmon flakes easily and a thermometer reads 125°, 14-18 minutes. Cut salmon into 4 equal portions.

1 FILLET: 295 cal., 19g fat (4g sat. fat), 85mg chol., 380mg sod., 0 carb. (0 sugars, 0 fiber), 29g pro. **DIABETIC EXCHANGES:** 4 lean meat, ½ fat.

LEVEL IT UP WITH AN EASY TOPPER

- **Gremolata:** In a small bowl, mix ¼ cup minced fresh parsley, 2 Tbsp. olive oil, 1 Tbsp. lemon juice, 1 minced garlic clove, 1 tsp. grated lemon zest, ½ tsp. salt and ¼ tsp. pepper.

- **Dill And Caper Butter:** In a small bowl, mix ¼ cup softened butter, 1 Tbsp. minced shallot, 1 Tbsp. minced fresh dill, 1 tsp. Dijon mustard and 1 tsp. chopped capers.

- **Maple Soy Glaze:** In a small bowl, mix ¼ cup maple syrup, 2 Tbsp. soy sauce, 1 minced green onion, ½ tsp. grated fresh ginger and ¼ tsp. red pepper flakes.

NICOISE SALAD

This garden-fresh salad is a feast for the eyes as well as the palate. Add some French bread and you have a mouthwatering meal.
—Marla Fogderud, Mason, MI

PREP: 40 MIN. + COOLING • **MAKES:** 2 SERVINGS

⅓ cup olive oil
3 Tbsp. white wine vinegar
1½ tsp. Dijon mustard
⅛ tsp. each salt, onion powder and pepper

SALAD
2 small red potatoes
½ cup cut fresh green beans

3½ cups torn Bibb lettuce
½ cup cherry tomatoes, halved
10 Greek olives, pitted and halved
2 hard-boiled large eggs, quartered
1 can (5 oz.) albacore white tuna in water, drained and flaked

1. In a small bowl, whisk the oil, vinegar, mustard, salt, onion powder and pepper; set aside.

2. Place potatoes in a small saucepan and cover with water. Bring to a boil. Reduce heat; cover and simmer until tender, 15-20 minutes. Drain and cool; cut into quarters.

3. Place beans in another saucepan and cover with water. Bring to a boil. Cover and cook until crisp-tender, 3-5 minutes; drain and rinse in cold water.

4. Divide lettuce between 2 salad plates; top with potatoes, beans, tomatoes, olives, eggs and tuna. Drizzle with dressing.

1 SERVING: 613 cal., 49g fat (8g sat. fat), 242mg chol., 886mg sod., 18g carb. (3g sugars, 3g fiber), 26g pro.

HOW TO BLANCH GREEN BEANS

Use this chef's technique for perfect brilliant green, flavorful and crisp-tender beans. They're ideal for tossing in a salad or for preparing in advance to quickly reheat later.

Blanching in hot water cooks the beans and shocking in ice water sets the vibrant green color and stops the cooking process.

For 1 lb. of green beans, bring 1 qt. water and 1 Tbsp. salt to a boil. Add beans; cook until beans are just tender, 3-5 minutes. Transfer beans to a bowl of ice water; let cool. Remove beans from water and pat dry.

MAKE HARD-COOKED EGGS (5 DIFFERENT WAYS)

Just hover your camera here.

GARLIC LEMON SHRIMP

This shrimp dish is amazingly quick to get on the table. Serve it with crusty bread so you can soak up the luscious garlic lemon sauce.
—Athena Russell, Greenville, SC

TAKES: 20 MIN. • **MAKES:** 4 SERVINGS

2 Tbsp. olive oil	1 Tbsp. lemon juice
1 lb. uncooked shrimp (26-30 per lb.), peeled and deveined	1 tsp. ground cumin
	¼ tsp. salt
3 garlic cloves, thinly sliced	2 Tbsp. minced fresh parsley
	Hot cooked pasta or rice

In a large cast-iron or other heavy skillet, heat oil over medium-high heat; saute shrimp 3 minutes. Add garlic, lemon juice, cumin and salt; cook and stir until shrimp turn pink, 2-3 minutes. Stir in parsley. Serve with pasta.

1 SERVING: 163 cal., 8g fat (1g sat. fat), 138mg chol., 284mg sod., 2g carb. (0 sugars, 0 fiber), 19g pro. **DIABETIC EXCHANGES:** 3 lean meat, 1½ fat.

HEALTH TIP

Cooking the shrimp in olive oil instead of butter saves about 3 grams of saturated fat per serving.

HOW TO TELL IF SHRIMP ARE PERFECTLY COOKED

Uncooked shrimp will turn from gray or white and translucent to pink and opaque when cooked, and from soft to firm. The tails, if left on, will be dark pink.

Raw: Relaxed shape and raw interior.

Perfectly Cooked: Flesh in the middle is firm and opaque, but still has a sheen (as opposed to matte white).

Overcooked: Has tightly coiled shape. Interior has visibly lost moisture and the fibers are constricted.

POULTRY

Chicken and turkey are always great choices, whether it's simple fried chicken or a roasted holiday turkey with all the trimmings. Here you'll discover family-pleasing nuggets, Jamaican jerk turkey wraps and panini just like a sandwich shop's.

HERB CHICKEN WITH HONEY BUTTER

When the whole family could use a heartwarming meal, this one is ideal. You'll love how the honey's sweetness mixes perfectly with the herbs' salty flavor. It's a wonderful combination!
—*Taste of Home* Test Kitchen

TAKES: 25 MIN. • **MAKES:** 4 SERVINGS

1 large egg, lightly beaten	4 boneless skinless chicken
¾ cup seasoned bread crumbs	breast halves (6 oz. each)
2 Tbsp. dried parsley flakes	3 Tbsp. butter
1 tsp. Italian seasoning	
¾ tsp. garlic salt	HONEY BUTTER
½ tsp. poultry seasoning	¼ cup butter, softened
	¼ cup honey

1. Place egg in a shallow bowl. In another shallow bowl, combine the bread crumbs and seasonings. Dip chicken in egg, then coat with the bread crumb mixture.

2. Heat a large cast-iron or other heavy skillet over medium heat. Cook chicken in butter until a thermometer reads 165°, 4-5 minutes on each side. Meanwhile, combine softened butter and honey. Serve with chicken.

1 CHICKEN BREAST HALF WITH 2 TBSP. HONEY BUTTER: 485 cal., 25g fat (14g sat. fat), 171mg chol., 709mg sod., 27g carb. (18g sugars, 1g fiber), 38g pro.

BUTTER UP!

Start with 1 stick of softened butter, then stir in these seasonings. Use to flavor chicken, veggie sautes, corn on the cob and more.

- **New York:** ⅓ cup chopped fresh basil, ½ tsp. lemon juice, ½ tsp. seasoned pepper and ¼ tsp. garlic salt

- **California-Style:** 2 tsp. minced fresh rosemary and 1 Tbsp. minced black olives

- **Southwest:** ½ tsp. ground chipotle pepper, zest of 1 lime and 1 tsp. minced cilantro

- **Heartland:** 2 Tbsp. crumbled Maytag blue cheese

- **East Coast:** 2 tsp. Old Bay seasoning and zest of 1 lemon

- **Dairy State:** 2 Tbsp. grated Parmesan cheese and 2 Tbsp. finely shredded cheddar cheese

PREPARE & FREEZE FLAVORED BUTTER

Step 1: Place butter on a square of parchment, mounding butter into a rough log shape.

Step 2: Fold paper toward you, enclosing the butter. Press butter with a ruler to form a log, holding the edges of paper securely with the other hand. Twist edges to seal. Wrap butter in plastic and freeze. Slice off the desired portions when ready to use, then rewrap the butter and return it to the freezer.

Step 3: You can also freeze scoops or rosettes of flavored butter on a parchment paper-lined baking sheet. Once frozen, arrange the butter portions on layers of paper in a freezer container. Remove the desired number of portions from the freezer when needed.

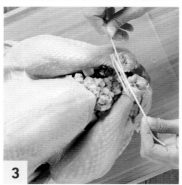

HOW TO STUFF A WHOLE TURKEY

Step 1: Tuck wing tips under body to aid in even cooking.

Step 2: Combine stuffing as the recipe directs, but do not stuff the turkey until you're ready to place it in the oven. When you're ready to cook the bird, spoon the stuffing loosely into the cavity.

Step 3: Tie drumsticks together with kitchen string.

CLASSIC STUFFED TURKEY

This moist dressing features fresh mushrooms, and its flavor nicely complements the tender and juicy slices of oven-roasted turkey.
—Kathi Graham, Naperville, IL

PREP: 20 MIN. • **BAKE:** 3¾ HOURS + STANDING
MAKES: 12 SERVINGS (10 CUPS STUFFING)

2 **large onions, chopped**	1 **tsp. poultry seasoning**
2 **celery ribs, chopped**	½ **tsp. pepper**
½ **lb. fresh mushrooms, sliced**	12 **cups unseasoned stuffing**
½ **cup butter**	**cubes**
1 **can (14½ oz.) chicken broth**	**Warm water**
⅓ **cup minced fresh parsley**	1 **turkey (14 to 16 lbs.)**
2 **tsp. rubbed sage**	**Melted butter**
1 **tsp. salt**	

1. In a large skillet, saute the onions, celery and mushrooms in butter until tender. Add broth and seasonings; mix well. Place bread cubes in a large bowl; add mushroom mixture and toss to coat. Stir in enough warm water to reach desired moistness.

2. Just before baking, loosely stuff turkey. Place any remaining stuffing in a greased baking dish; cover and refrigerate until ready to bake. Skewer turkey openings; tie drumsticks together with kitchen string. Place breast side up on a rack in a roasting pan. Brush with melted butter.

3. Bake the turkey, uncovered, at 325° for 3¾-4½ hours or until a thermometer reads 165° when inserted in center of stuffing and the thigh reaches at least 170°, basting occasionally with pan drippings. (Cover loosely with foil if turkey browns too quickly.)

4. Bake additional stuffing, covered, for 30-40 minutes. Uncover; bake 10 minutes longer or until lightly browned. Cover turkey with foil and let stand for 20 minutes before removing stuffing and carving. If desired, thicken pan drippings for gravy.

1 SERVING: 571 cal., 26g fat (11g sat. fat), 153mg chol., 961mg sod., 42g carb. (5g sugars, 4g fiber), 44g pro.

TEST KITCHEN TIP

Make this stuffing your own with 1 of more of these mix-in ideas: chopped pecans, crumbled cooked sausage or bacon, sauteed chopped apples and dried cranberries.

SEASONED CHICKEN STRIPS

I made these crisp chicken strips for my kids, but they're tasty enough for company. They're juicy and flavorful and would also be a great salad topper.
—Becky Oliver, Fairplay, CO

TAKES: 25 MIN. • **MAKES:** 4 SERVINGS

- ⅓ cup egg substitute or 1 large egg
- 1 Tbsp. prepared mustard
- 1 garlic clove, minced
- ¾ cup dry bread crumbs
- 2 tsp. dried basil
- 1 tsp. paprika
- ½ tsp. salt
- ¼ tsp. pepper
- 1 lb. chicken tenderloins

1. Preheat oven to 400°. In a shallow bowl, whisk together egg substitute, mustard and garlic. In another shallow bowl, toss bread crumbs with seasonings. Dip chicken in egg mixture, then coat with crumb mixture.

2. Place on a baking sheet coated with cooking spray. Bake until golden brown and chicken is no longer pink, 10-15 minutes.

3 OZ. COOKED CHICKEN: 194 cal., 2g fat (0 sat. fat), 56mg chol., 518mg sod., 14g carb. (1g sugars, 1g fiber), 31g pro. **DIABETIC EXCHANGES:** 3 lean meat, 1 starch.

CRISPY TORTILLA CHICKEN

Finely crush tortilla chips to use in place of the bread crumbs. Replace basil with ½ tsp. dried oregano and ¼ tsp. ground cumin. Proceed as directed. Serve chicken with salsa or sour cream.

DIY BBQ SAUCE
It's easy and fun to create your own fruit-kissed BBQ dippers. Start with **1 cup BBQ sauce** and add:

Cranberry BBQ Sauce:
- 1 cup whole-berry cranberry sauce, heated
- ¾ tsp. each ground cinnamon, cumin, pepper and chili powder
- ¼ tsp. salt

Pineapple BBQ Sauce:
- 1 8-oz. can crushed pineapple, undrained
- ⅓ cup finely chopped onion
- 2 Tbsp. chili sauce

Berry Patch BBQ Sauce:
- 1½ cups each blackberries and blueberries
- ⅓ cup sugar
- 3 Tbsp. water

Simmer until thickened, then add BBQ sauce.

LEARN TO PREPARE TURKEY CUTLETS

Just hover your camera here.

TURKEY CUTLETS WITH PAN GRAVY

Using cutlets or any boneless meat speeds up cooking time for this quick entree. You can use thin boneless, skinless chicken breast as well.
—Margaret Wilson, San Bernardino, CA

TAKES: 20 MIN. • **MAKES:** 4 SERVINGS

1 pkg. (20 oz.) turkey breast tenderloins	2 Tbsp. canola oil
1 tsp. poultry seasoning	2 Tbsp. butter
¼ tsp. seasoned salt	¼ cup all-purpose flour
¼ tsp. pepper, divided	2 cups chicken broth

1. Cut tenderloins crosswise into 1-in. slices; flatten slices with a meat mallet to ½-in. thickness. Mix poultry seasoning, seasoned salt and ⅛ tsp. pepper; sprinkle over turkey.

2. In a large skillet, heat oil over medium-high heat. Add turkey in batches; cook until no longer pink, 2-3 minutes per side. Remove from the pan; keep warm.

3. In same pan, melt butter over medium heat; stir in flour until smooth. Gradually stir in broth. Bring to a boil; cook and stir until thickened, about 2 minutes. Sprinkle with remaining ⅛ tsp. pepper. Serve with turkey.

1 SERVING: 292 cal., 15g fat (5g sat. fat), 89mg chol., 772mg sod., 7g carb. (1g sugars, 0 fiber), 31g pro. **DIABETIC EXCHANGES:** 4 lean meat, 3 fat, ½ starch.

EASY LEMON-ROSEMARY CHICKEN

This slow-cooked chicken is perfect for spring gatherings with its light and fresh lemon and rosemary flavor. It pairs well with a variety of sides, too. I love that the slow cooker does most of the work!
—Courtney Stultz, Weir, KS

PREP: 15 MIN. • **COOK:** 4 HOURS + STANDING • **MAKES:** 6 SERVINGS

- 1 broiler/fryer chicken (3 to 4 lbs.)
- 2 celery ribs, cut into 1-in. pieces
- 1 medium onion, chopped
- 1 medium apple, sliced
- 1 Tbsp. olive oil
- 1 Tbsp. minced fresh rosemary or 1 tsp. dried rosemary, crushed
- 2 tsp. sea salt
- 1½ tsp. minced fresh thyme or ½ tsp. dried thyme
- 1½ tsp. paprika
- 1 garlic clove, minced
- 1 tsp. pepper
- 1 medium lemon, sliced

1. Fill chicken cavity with celery, onion and apple. Tuck wings under chicken; tie drumsticks together. Place in a 6-qt. slow cooker, breast side up. Rub chicken with oil; rub with rosemary, salt, thyme, paprika, garlic and pepper. Top with lemon.

2. Cook, covered, on low until a thermometer inserted in thickest part of thigh reads at least 170°-175°, 4-5 hours. Remove chicken from slow cooker; tent with foil. Discard vegetables and apple. Let chicken stand 15 minutes before carving.

5 OZ. COOKED CHICKEN: 318 cal., 19g fat (5g sat. fat), 104mg chol., 730mg sod., 1g carb. (0 sugars, 0 fiber), 33g pro.

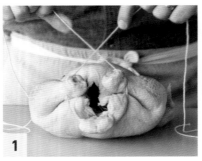
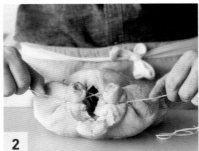
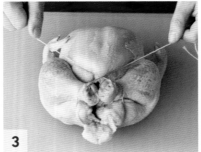
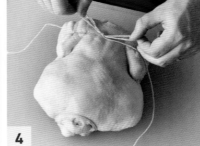

HOW TO TRUSS A CHICKEN

Step 1: Place aromatics in bird, if using. Place kitchen twine under the tail and loop around the ankles, pulling up tightly.

Step 2: After making an "X" with the string, reverse your grip on the twine and cross the ends down and around the ankles in a figure-8 pattern. Pull tightly so the legs move together: The goal is to create a tight, compact shape.

Step 3: Pull twine up around the thighs and hook it under the wing joints.

Step 4: Flip the chicken and tie the twine in a firm knot. Tuck wings under bird and trim any excess twine.

SWEET POTATO-CRUSTED CHICKEN NUGGETS

I was looking for ways to spice up traditional chicken nuggets and came up with this recipe. The chips add a crunchy texture and flavor, while the meat is tender on the inside.
—Kristina Segarra, Yonkers, NY

TAKES: 30 MIN. • **MAKES:** 4 SERVINGS

Oil for deep-fat frying
1 cup sweet potato chips
¼ cup all-purpose flour
1 tsp. salt, divided
½ tsp. coarsely ground pepper
¼ tsp. baking powder
1 Tbsp. cornstarch
1 lb. chicken tenderloins, cut into 1½-in. pieces

1. In an electric skillet or deep fryer, heat oil to 350°. Place chips, flour, ½ tsp. salt, pepper and baking powder in a food processor; pulse until ground. Transfer to a shallow dish.

2. Mix cornstarch and remaining ½ tsp. salt; toss with chicken. Toss with potato chip mixture, pressing gently to coat.

3. Fry nuggets, a few at a time, until golden brown, 2-3 minutes. Drain on paper towels.

1 SERVING: 308 cal., 17g fat (1g sat. fat), 56mg chol., 690mg sod., 12g carb. (1g sugars, 1g fiber), 28g pro.

AIR-FRIED VARIATION

Preheat air fryer to 400°. Prepare chicken as directed.

In batches, arrange chicken in a single layer on greased tray in air-fryer basket; spritz with cooking spray. Cook until golden brown, 3-4 minutes. Turn; spritz with cooking spray. Cook until golden brown and chicken is no longer pink, 3-4 minutes longer.

MAKE YOUR OWN DIPPING SAUCES
If you're a dunker, serve the nuggets with a yummy sauce.

Sweet-and-Sour Sauce:
- ½ cup orange marmalade
- 2 Tbsp. white vinegar
- 1 Tbsp. diced pimientos
- ⅛ tsp. paprika
- Dash salt

Combine all ingredients in a small bowl; cover and refrigerate until serving.

Honey-Mustard Dipper:
- ½ cup Dijon mustard
- ½ cup honey
- ¼ cup soy sauce
- 2 tsp. sugar

Combine all ingredients in a small bowl; cover and refrigerate until serving.

Copycat Chick-fil-A Sauce:
- 5 Tbsp. mayonnaise
- ¼ cup Dijon mustard
- 3 Tbsp. BBQ sauce
- 3 Tbsp. honey

Combine all ingredients in a small bowl; cover and refrigerate until serving.

CHICKEN FLORENTINE PANINI

This grilled sandwich combines chicken with provolone cheese, spinach and red onion.
—Lee Bremson, Kansas City, MO

TAKES: 25 MIN. • **MAKES:** 4 SERVINGS

- 1 pkg. (5 oz.) fresh baby spinach
- 2 tsp. olive oil
- ¼ cup butter, softened
- 8 slices sourdough bread
- ¼ cup creamy Italian salad dressing
- 8 slices provolone cheese
- ½ lb. shaved deli chicken
- 2 slices red onion, separated into rings

1. In a large cast-iron or other heavy skillet, saute spinach in oil until wilted, about 2 minutes. Drain; wipe skillet clean.

2. Spread 4 bread slices with salad dressing. Layer with a cheese slice, chicken, spinach, onion and another cheese slice. Top with remaining bread. Butter outsides of sandwiches.

3. Cook in the same skillet or panini maker until bread is golden brown and cheese is melted.

1 SANDWICH: 582 cal., 26g fat (10g sat. fat), 62mg chol., 1688mg sod., 63g carb. (4g sugars, 5g fiber), 23g pro.

PANINI PRESS FROM CAST-IRON SKILLETS

Step 1: Preheat 2 cast-iron skillets, preferably 1 slightly smaller than the other, over medium-high heat. Add canola or olive oil to the bottom skillet before adding your assembled sandwich. Wipe the bottom of the second skillet with oil, then place it on top of the sandwich.

Step 2: Press firmly and then place a heat-safe weight, such as a filled tea kettle, in the skillet. Cook for about 4 minutes or until the sandwich is golden brown. If necessary, flip sandwiches to ensure they're toasted on both sides.

JAMAICAN JERK TURKEY WRAPS

After tasting these spicy wraps at a neighborhood party, I got the recipe.
The grilled turkey tenderloin and light jalapeno dressing make them a hit.
—Mary Ann Dell, Phoenixville, PA

PREP: 20 MIN. • **GRILL:** 20 MIN. • **MAKES:** 4 WRAPS

- 2 cups broccoli coleslaw mix
- 1 medium tomato, seeded and chopped
- 3 Tbsp. reduced-fat coleslaw dressing
- 1 jalapeno pepper, seeded and chopped
- 1 Tbsp. prepared mustard
- 1½ tsp. Caribbean jerk seasoning
- 2 turkey breast tenderloins (8 oz. each)
- 4 flour tortillas (8 in.)

1. In a large bowl, toss coleslaw mix, tomato, coleslaw dressing, jalapeno and mustard.

2. Rub seasoning over turkey tenderloins. On a greased grill, cook turkey, covered, over medium heat or broil 4 in. from heat until a thermometer reads 165°, 8-10 minutes on each side. Let stand 5 minutes.

3. Grill the tortillas, uncovered, over medium heat until they're warmed, 45-55 seconds on each side. Thinly slice turkey; place down the center of tortillas. Top with coleslaw mixture and roll up.

1 WRAP: 343 cal., 8g fat (1g sat. fat), 48mg chol., 654mg sod., 37g carb. (7g sugars, 3g fiber), 34g pro. **DIABETIC EXCHANGES:** 3 lean meat, 2 starch, 1 vegetable, ½ fat.

SWEET, SPICY JERK SEASONING

Jerk seasoning is a blend of dried hot peppers, onion, garlic and thyme mixed with sweet spices, such as allspice and cinnamon. As with any spice blend, each will vary according to the manufacturer's recipe.

If you can't find jerk seasoning, mix up your own batch with spices you have on hand. Your goal: A flavor that's hot to your desired spice level and slightly sweet.

Team up the Jerk turkey wraps with Baked Potato Chips (p. 217) and.Frozen Coconut Margaritas (p. 22) for an impromptu tropical getaway!

IN-A-PINCH CHICKEN & SPINACH

I needed a fast supper while babysitting my grandchild. I used what my daughter-in-law had in the fridge and turned it into what's now one of our favorite recipes.
—Sandra Ellis, Stockbridge, GA

TAKES: 25 MIN. • **MAKES:** 4 SERVINGS

- 4 boneless skinless chicken breast halves (6 oz. each)
- 2 Tbsp. olive oil
- 1 Tbsp. butter
- 1 pkg. (6 oz.) fresh baby spinach
- 1 cup salsa

1. Pound chicken with a meat mallet to ½-in. thickness. In a large skillet, heat oil and butter over medium heat. Cook chicken until no longer pink, 5-6 minutes on each side. Remove and keep warm.

2. Add spinach and salsa to pan; cook and stir just until spinach is wilted, 3-4 minutes. Serve with chicken.

1 CHICKEN BREAST HALF WITH ⅓ CUP SPINACH MIXTURE: 297 cal., 14g fat (4g sat. fat), 102mg chol., 376mg sod., 6g carb. (2g sugars, 1g fiber), 36g pro. **DIABETIC EXCHANGES:** 5 lean meat, 2 fat, 1 vegetable.

MEAT MALLET SUBSTITUTE

Reach for a small to medium saucepan or small skillet if you don't have a meat mallet.

**PERFECTLY
TIME THAT
TURKEY**

Just hover your
camera here.

SEASONED ROAST TURKEY

Rubbing the skin with melted butter keeps this simply seasoned turkey moist and tender.
—Nancy Reichert, Thomasville, GA

PREP: 15 MIN. • **BAKE:** 2¾ HOURS + STANDING • **MAKES:** 15 SERVINGS

¼ cup butter, melted	1 tsp. ground ginger
2 tsp. salt	¾ tsp. pepper
2 tsp. garlic powder	½ tsp. dried basil
2 tsp. seasoned salt	¼ tsp. cayenne pepper
1½ tsp. paprika	1 turkey (13 to 15 lbs.)

1. Preheat oven to 325°. In a small bowl, combine the first 9 ingredients. Place turkey, breast side up, on a rack in a roasting pan; pat dry. Brush with butter mixture.

2. Bake, uncovered, until a thermometer inserted in thickest part of thigh reads 170°-175°, 2¾-3¼ hours. (Cover loosely with foil if turkey browns too quickly.) Cover and let stand 20 minutes before carving.

4 OZ. COOKED TURKEY: 488 cal., 24g fat (8g sat. fat), 221mg chol., 698mg sod., 1g carb. (0 sugars, 0 fiber), 63g pro.

SEASONED ROAST TURKEY TIPS

How can you tell when roast turkey is done? Your roast turkey is done when a thermometer inserted into the thickest part of the bird (usually the thigh) registers 170°-175°F (165°F for a turkey breast). Make sure the thermometer is not touching bone, which can give an inaccurate reading. If you do not have a thermometer, pierce the skin of the mid-thigh with a fork and pay attention to the juices. If the juices run clear, your turkey is done.

How do you keep a roast turkey from drying out? The key to perfectly moist and juicy turkey is to let it rest before carving. When you have removed the turkey from the oven, let it rest on the cutting board for at least 20 minutes to incorporate any juices back into the meat. Resist the temptation to baste your turkey, as every time you open the oven door, you are letting heat escape. This leads to a longer cook time, which can spell drier meat.

CHICKEN TAMALES

I love tamales. They take a little time but are so worth the effort. I usually make them for Christmas. My family wants them more often, so I freeze a big batch.
—Cindy Pruitt, Grove, OK

PREP: 2½ HOURS + SOAKING • **COOK:** 45 MIN. • **MAKES:** 20 TAMALES

- 24 **dried corn husks**
- 1 **broiler/fryer chicken (3 to 4 lbs.), cut up**
- 1 **medium onion, quartered**
- 2 **tsp. salt**
- 1 **garlic clove, crushed**
- 3 **qt. water**

DOUGH
- 1 **cup shortening**
- 3 **cups masa harina**

FILLING
- 6 **Tbsp. canola oil**
- 6 **Tbsp. all-purpose flour**
- ¾ **cup chili powder**
- ½ **tsp. salt**
- ¼ **tsp. garlic powder**
- ¼ **tsp. pepper**
- 2 **cans (2¼ oz. each) sliced ripe olives, drained**
- **Hot water**

1. Cover corn husks with cold water; soak until softened, at least 2 hours. Place chicken, onion, salt and garlic in a 6-qt. stockpot. Pour in 3 qt. water; bring to a boil. Reduce heat; simmer, covered, until chicken is tender, 45-60 minutes. Remove chicken from broth. When cool enough to handle, remove bones and skin; discard. Shred chicken. Strain cooking juices; skim off fat. Reserve 6 cups stock.

2. For dough, beat shortening until light and fluffy, about 1 minute. Beat in small amounts of masa harina alternately with small amounts of reserved stock, using no more than 2 cups stock. Drop a small amount of dough into a cup of cold water; dough should float. If not, continue beating, rechecking every 1-2 minutes.

3. For the filling, heat oil in a Dutch oven; stir in flour until blended. Cook and stir over medium heat until lightly browned, 7-9 minutes. Stir in seasonings, chicken and remaining stock; bring to a boil. Reduce heat; simmer, uncovered, until thick, about 45 minutes, stirring occasionally.

4. Drain corn husks and pat dry; tear 4 husks to make 20 strips for tying tamales. (To prevent husks from drying out, cover with a damp towel until ready to use.) On wide end of each remaining husk, spread 3 Tbsp. dough to within ½ in. of side edges; top each with 2 Tbsp. chicken filling and 2 tsp. olives. Fold long sides of husk over filling, overlapping slightly. Fold over narrow end of husk; tie with a strip of husk to secure.

5. Place a large steamer basket in the stockpot over water; place the tamales upright in steamer. Bring to a boil; steam, covered, adding water as needed, until dough peels away from husk, about 45 minutes.

2 TAMALES: 564 cal., 35g fat (7g sat. fat), 44mg chol., 835mg sod., 43g carb. (2g sugars, 7g fiber), 20g pro.

ABOUT TAMALE INGREDIENTS
Fresh masa (dough made from stone-ground corn flour, called masa harina) is the foundation of a perfect tamale. You can find masa harina and corn husks in the international foods aisle or online.

WATCH US
MAKE IT
Just hover your
camera here.

STUFFED CHICKEN ROLLS

Just thinking about this dish sparks my appetite. The ham and cheese rolled inside are a tasty surprise. Leftovers reheat well and make a perfect lunch with a green salad.
—Jean Sherwood, Kenneth City, FL

PREP: 25 MIN. + CHILLING • **COOK:** 4 HOURS • **MAKES:** 6 SERVINGS

- 6 boneless skinless chicken breast halves (8 oz. each)
- 6 slices fully cooked ham
- 6 slices Swiss cheese
- ¼ cup all-purpose flour
- ¼ cup grated Parmesan cheese
- ½ tsp. rubbed sage
- ¼ tsp. paprika
- ¼ tsp. pepper
- ¼ cup canola oil
- 1 can (10¾ oz.) condensed cream of chicken soup, undiluted
- ½ cup chicken broth
  Chopped fresh parsley, optional

1. Flatten each chicken breast half to ¼-in. thickness; top with ham and Swiss cheese. Roll up and tuck in ends; secure with toothpicks.

2. In a shallow bowl, combine the flour, Parmesan, sage, paprika and pepper; coat chicken on all sides. In a large skillet, brown chicken in oil over medium-high heat.

3. Transfer to a 5-qt. slow cooker. Combine soup and broth; pour over chicken. Cover and cook on low until chicken is tender, 4-5 hours. Remove toothpicks. Garnish with parsley if desired.

1 STUFFED CHICKEN BREAST HALF: 525 cal., 26g fat (10g sat. fat), 167mg chol., 914mg sod., 9g carb. (1g sugars, 1g fiber), 60g pro.

FREEZE OPTION

Cool chicken mixture. Freeze in freezer containers. To use, partially thaw in refrigerator overnight. Heat through slowly in a covered skillet, stirring occasionally, until a thermometer inserted in chicken reads 165°.

MAKE IT YOUR OWN
Fill these chicken rolls with just about anything!

Italian: Prosciutto, sliced mozzarella and fresh basil

French: mushrooms, leeks, Boursin garlic and fine herbs cheese

Mediterranean: Spinach, sun-dried tomatoes, fresh garlic and goat cheese

Mexican: Chorizo, cilantro and Monterey Jack cheese

Greek: Kalamata olives, chopped artichokes and capers, feta

American: Bacon, caramelized onion and Brie

PICNIC FRIED CHICKEN

For our family, it's not a picnic unless there's fried chicken! Chicken, deviled eggs and potato salad are all musts for a picnic as far as my husband is concerned. This is a golden oldie recipe for me—I've used it many times through the years.
—Edna Hoffman, Hebron, IN

PREP: 30 MIN. + MARINATING • **COOK:** 40 MIN. • **MAKES:** 6 SERVINGS

1 broiler/fryer chicken (3 lbs.), cut up
¾ to 1 cup buttermilk

COATING
1½ to 2 cups all-purpose flour
1½ tsp. salt
½ tsp. pepper
½ tsp. garlic powder
½ tsp. onion powder
1 Tbsp. paprika
¼ tsp. ground sage
¼ tsp. ground thyme
⅛ tsp. baking powder
Oil for frying

1. Pat chicken with paper towels; place in large flat dish. Pour buttermilk over chicken; cover and refrigerate at least 1 hour or overnight.

2. Combine flour, seasonings and baking powder in a large shallow dish or resealable plastic bag. Add chicken pieces, 1 at a time, and turn to coat. Lay coated pieces on waxed paper for 15 minutes to allow coating to dry (this will help the coating cling during frying).

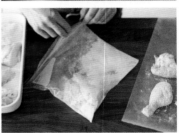

3. In a Dutch oven or deep skillet, heat ½ in. oil over medium heat to 350°. Fry chicken in batches, uncovered, turning occasionally, until coating is a dark golden brown and meat is no longer pink, 7-8 minutes per side. Drain on paper towels.

5 OZ. COOKED CHICKEN: 623 cal., 40g fat (7g sat. fat), 106mg chol., 748mg sod., 26g carb. (2g sugars, 1g fiber), 38g pro.

FRIED CHICKEN POINTERS

- Acidic buttermilk tenderizes the chicken, but plain yogurt will work, too.

- For a crispy coating that stays put after frying, allow excess buttermilk to drip off before coating chicken in the flour mixture.

- To keep fried chicken crunchy, we recommend storing it on a wire rack. No more soggy bottoms!

HOW TO CARVE A CHICKEN

Step 1: Let chicken stand at least 15 minutes before carving. Place chicken on a cutting board. Using a carving fork to stabilize the chicken, cut through the skin, separating the leg from the body.

Step 2: Continue cutting down through the hip joint to remove the leg and thigh (also called a leg quarter) in 1 piece. Jiggle the leg to free it from the joint if necessary. Repeat on the second side.

Step 3: Separate drumsticks and thighs by cutting through the joint of each leg quarter.

Step 4: To remove the breast meat, first make a horizontal cut near the base of the chicken toward its center.

Step 5: Next, cut down along the breastbone, through to the horizontal cut that was just made. Remove the entire breast half. Rotate the chicken 180° and reposition the carving fork. Repeat on the second side to remove remaining breast half.

Step 6: Slice the chicken breast meat as desired.

Step 7: Pull wings away from the body. For an attractive presentation, cut away and discard the wing tips.

Step 8: Plate chicken and serve.

GET MORE CARVING BASICS
Just hover your camera here.

ROTISSERIE-STYLE CHICKEN

*My mother used to fix this chicken when I lived at home, and we called it Church Chicken
because Mom would put it in the oven Sunday morning before we left for church.
When we got home, the aroma of the roasted chicken would hit us as we opened the door.*
—Brian Stevenson, Grand Rapids, MI

PREP: 15 MIN. + CHILLING • **BAKE:** 1¼ HOURS + STANDING • **MAKES:** 6 SERVINGS

 2 tsp. salt
1¼ tsp. paprika
 1 tsp. brown sugar
 ¾ tsp. dried thyme
 ¾ tsp. white pepper
 ¼ tsp. cayenne pepper
 ¼ tsp. pepper
 1 broiler/fryer chicken
    (3 to 4 lbs.)
 1 medium onion, quartered

1. Mix the first 7 ingredients. Rub over the outside and inside of chicken. Place in a large dish. Cover and refrigerate 8 hours or overnight.

2. Preheat oven to 350°. Place chicken on a rack in a shallow roasting pan, breast side up. Tuck wings under chicken; tie drumsticks together. Place onion around chicken in pan.

3. Roast until a thermometer inserted in thickest part of thigh reads 170°-175°, 1¼-1½ hours. Baste occasionally with pan drippings. (Cover loosely with foil if chicken browns too quickly.)

4. Remove chicken from oven; tent with foil. Let stand 15 minutes before slicing.

5 OZ. COOKED CHICKEN: 306 cal., 17g fat (5g sat. fat), 104mg chol., 878mg sod., 3g carb. (2g sugars, 1g fiber), 33g pro.

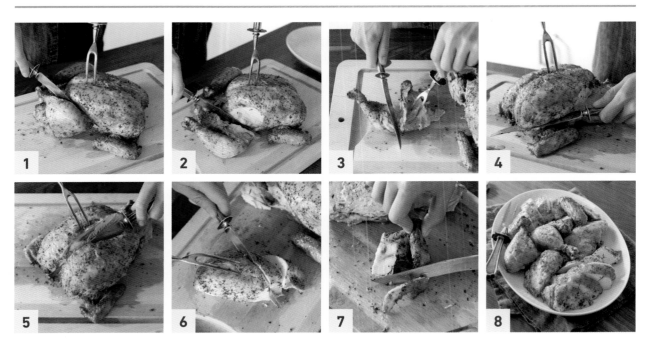

TURKEY A LA KING

This is a smart way to use up leftover turkey. You might want to make a double batch!
—Mary Gaylord, Balsam Lake, WI

TAKES: 25 MIN. • **MAKES:** 6 SERVINGS

- 1 medium onion, chopped
- ¾ cup sliced celery
- ¼ cup diced green pepper
- ¼ cup butter, cubed
- ¼ cup all-purpose flour
- 1 tsp. sugar
- 1½ cups chicken broth
- ¼ cup half-and-half cream
- 3 cups cubed cooked turkey or chicken
- 1 can (4 oz.) sliced mushrooms, drained
- 6 slices bread, toasted

1. In a large skillet, saute the onion, celery and green pepper in butter until tender. Stir in flour and sugar until a paste forms.

2. Gradually stir in broth. Bring to a boil; boil until thickened, about 1 minute. Reduce heat. Add cream, turkey and mushrooms; heat through. Serve with toast.

1 SERVING: 297 cal., 13g fat (7g sat. fat), 98mg chol., 591mg sod., 21g carb. (4g sugars, 2g fiber), 24g pro.

MAKE IT YOUR OWN

Turkey (or chicken) a la king is a dish steeped in history, with many wonderful variations. Consider these additions to create your own classic.

- **Sherry:** A splash of sherry (use ¼ cup and decrease the chicken broth accordingly) would add rich flavor and complexity. Cooking sherry is just fine for this.

- **Pimientos:** Adding a well-drained small jar of the bright red peppers is considered classic by many. Stir in right at the end.

- **Peas:** Stir in ½ cup frozen peas near the end of cooking for a burst of color.

- **Mashed Potatoes, Biscuits, Noodles or Puff Pastry Cups:** Toast is expedient, but it's not the only starch in town when it comes to serving the rich stew.

SEE HOW WE
MADE IT
Just hover your
camera here.

CHEESY CHICKEN PARMIGIANA

My husband used to order chicken parmigiana at restaurants. Then I found this recipe in our local newspaper, adjusted it for two and began making the beloved dish at home. After more than 50 years of marriage, I still enjoy preparing his favorite recipes.
—Iola Butler, Sun City, CA

PREP: 25 MIN. • **COOK:** 15 MIN. • **MAKES:** 2 SERVINGS

- 1 **can (15 oz.) tomato sauce**
- 2 **tsp. Italian seasoning**
- ½ **tsp. garlic powder**
- 1 **large egg**
- ¼ **cup seasoned bread crumbs**
- 3 **Tbsp. grated Parmesan cheese**
- 2 **boneless skinless chicken breast halves (4 oz. each)**
- 2 **Tbsp. olive oil**
- 2 **slices part-skim mozzarella cheese**
  Optional: Fresh basil leaves and additional Parmesan cheese

1. In a small saucepan, combine the tomato sauce, Italian seasoning and garlic powder. Bring to a boil. Reduce heat; cover and simmer for 20 minutes.

2. Meanwhile, in a shallow bowl, lightly beat the egg. In another shallow bowl, combine bread crumbs and Parmesan cheese. Dip chicken in egg, then coat with crumb mixture.

3. In a large skillet, cook chicken in oil over medium heat until a thermometer reads 165°, about 5 minutes on each side. Top with mozzarella cheese. Cover and cook until cheese is melted, 3-4 minutes longer. Serve with tomato sauce. If desired, sprinkle with basil and additional Parmesan.

1 CHICKEN BREAST HALF: 444 cal., 26g fat (8g sat. fat), 166mg chol., 1496mg sod., 23g carb. (5g sugars, 3g fiber), 29g pro.

CHICKEN PARM SERVING IDEAS

- Serve the chicken over angel hair pasta for a quick and satisfying meal.

- Cut chicken breasts in half; place on toasted buns to make sliders.

- Team up the chicken with Antipasto Platter (p. 26) and Garden Vegetable & Herb Soup (p. 46) for an easy Italian feast.

BEEF

What's for dinner? Oftentimes, it's beef—whether you choose a quick skillet dish using a pound of ground beef or a New Year's Eve-worthy standing rib roast. No matter your level of expertise, you will find new dishes to challenge, inspire and delight.

QUICK & EASY SKILLET LASAGNA

This is a relatively new recipe to our family. We have made it quite a few times over the past few months. It's the perfect solution when you feel like lasagna but don't have time to bake it! You can also vary the taste depending on the type of pasta sauce or Italian dressing you use. Serve with salad or garlic bread.
—Wendy Masters, East Garafraxa, ON

TAKES: 30 MIN. • **MAKES:** 6 SERVINGS

- 1 **lb. lean ground beef (90% lean)**
- 1 **jar (24 oz.) pasta sauce**
- 2 **cups water**
- 1 **large sweet red pepper, chopped**
- ¼ **cup Italian salad dressing**
- 1 **tsp. garlic powder**
- 10 **uncooked lasagna noodles, broken into 2-in. pieces**
- 1½ **cups 2% cottage cheese**
- 1 **cup shredded part-skim mozzarella cheese**

1. In a large skillet, cook beef over medium heat until no longer pink; drain. Stir in pasta sauce, water, red pepper, dressing and garlic powder. Bring to a boil; stir in lasagna noodles. Reduce heat to medium-low. Cook, covered, until noodles are tender, 10-15 minutes, stirring occasionally.

2. Stir in cottage cheese; heat through. Remove from heat; top with mozzarella cheese. Cover and let stand until cheese is melted, about 5 minutes.

1 SERVING: 462 cal., 15g fat (6g sat. fat), 62mg chol., 857mg sod., 49g carb. (15g sugars, 5g fiber), 32g pro.

HOW TO COOK PASTA AL DENTE

The Italian phrase *al dente* literally translates to "to the tooth." It describes the texture of pasta that is tender but still firm and chewy when you bite into it. If the pasta is mushy, soft or falling apart, you've blasted right past al dente and into the overcooked zone.

The best way to test if pasta is al dente is to take a bite. About 2 minutes before the recommended time on the package directions, give the pasta a taste. If it's tender enough to chew but still contains a bit of a bite, you've reached al dente. If it's too firm for your liking, continue cooking until it reaches your preferred level of doneness.

GET 102
RECIPES
THAT USE
1 POUND OF
GROUND BEEF
Just hover your
camera here.

SHEET-PAN STEAK DINNER

Asparagus and steak form a classic combination for a delicious dinner. Cooking them together makes for easy prep and cleanup. In our house, any meal that can be put in the oven while we get a few more things done is a win!
—Estelle Forrest, Springfield, OR

PREP: 15 MIN. • **BAKE:** 25 MIN. • **MAKES:** 4 SERVINGS

1 tsp. minced fresh rosemary	1 lb. fresh asparagus, trimmed
½ tsp. each salt, pepper, paprika and garlic powder	2 Tbsp. avocado oil
1½ lbs. beef flank steak	2 Tbsp. butter, melted
	1 garlic clove, minced

1. Preheat oven to 400°. In small bowl, combine the rosemary and seasonings; set aside.

2. Place steak on 1 half of a 15x10x1-in. baking pan; place asparagus on the remaining half in a single layer. Brush steak with oil and sprinkle with seasoning mix. Combine butter and garlic, pour over asparagus.

3. Cover with foil; bake until meat reaches desired doneness (for medium-rare, a thermometer should read 135°, medium, 140°; medium-well, 145°), 25-30 minutes. Let steak stand 5-10 minutes before slicing. Serve with asparagus.

5 OZ. COOKED BEEF WITH 8 ASPARAGUS SPEARS: 380 cal., 25g fat (10g sat. fat), 96mg chol., 448mg sod., 3g carb. (1g sugars, 1g fiber), 34g pro.

SHEET-PAN STEAK TIPS

What other kinds of steak can you use to make sheet-pan steak? Flank steak is a lean cut, so don't use a cut that requires low-and-slow cooking or one that's perfect for just high-heat grilling. Instead, try skirt steak, flap steak, bavette or flat iron steak.

What other vegetables can you make with sheet-pan steak? Beef and asparagus make a classic pairing, but do you know what else does? Beef and potatoes! Cube or cut them into wedges. Roast a head of garlic and smear it on bread as a delectable side.

Mushrooms, peppers (think poblanos!), red onions, broccoli, Brussels sprouts or anything else you can cook on a sheet pan would be a nice addition to this meal. Keep in mind that different vegetables may have different cooking times (see sidebar at right).

BUILD THE PERFECT SHEET-PAN DINNER:
Sheet-pan dinners are a quick and easy way to put a healthy meal on the table. Follow these tips to whip up dinner in a flash.

- Invest in a good-quality sheet pan.

- Line the pan with foil for easy cleanup.

- Don't forget to toss the ingredients with a little oil first.

- Season generously.

- Don't overcrowd the pan.

- Elevate the ingredients on an ovenproof wire cooling rack to crisp things up.

- Give hearty vegetables (like potatoes or winter squash) a head start before adding other ingredients.

- Rotate the pan halfway through cooking.

SALT-ENCRUSTED RIB ROAST

A rib roast is a big part of our holiday dinner traditions. We love the yellow mustard, but you can use your favorite—Dijon and others are fair game.
—Rebecca Wirtzberger, Yuma, AZ

PREP: 15 MIN. • **BAKE:** 2½ HOURS + STANDING • **MAKES:** 10 SERVINGS

1 **bone-in beef rib roast** (about 6 lbs.)	3 **cups kosher salt** (about 1½ lbs.)
½ **cup yellow mustard**	½ **cup water**

1. Preheat oven to 450°. Place rib roast in a roasting pan, fat side up; spread all sides with mustard. In a bowl, mix salt and water to make a dry paste (mixture should be just moist enough to pack); press onto top and sides of roast.

2. Roast 15 minutes. Reduce oven setting to 325°. Roast 2¼-2¾ hours longer or until a thermometer inserted in beef reaches 135° for medium-rare; 140° for medium; 145° for medium-well. (Temperature of roast will continue to rise about 10° upon standing.) Let stand 20 minutes before serving.

3. Remove and discard salt crust. Carve roast into slices.

5 OZ. COOKED BEEF: 320 cal., 18g fat (7g sat. fat), 0 chol., 997mg sod., 1g carb. (0 sugars, 0 fiber), 37g pro.

HOME-STYLE GLAZED MEAT LOAF

Grated carrots and cheese add a hint of color to this down-home glazed meat loaf. We look forward to meat loaf sandwiches the next day!
—Sandra Etelamaki, Ishpeming, MI

PREP: 15 MIN. • **BAKE:** 1 HOUR + STANDING • **MAKES:** 12 SERVINGS

2 **large eggs, beaten**	¼ **tsp. garlic powder**
⅔ **cup 2% milk**	¼ **tsp. pepper**
1½ **cups shredded cheddar cheese**	2 **lbs. lean ground beef**
1 **cup crushed saltines (about 30 crackers)**	½ **cup packed brown sugar**
1 **cup finely shredded carrots**	½ **cup ketchup**
½ **cup finely chopped onion**	2 **Tbsp. Dijon mustard**
½ **tsp. salt**	**Minced fresh parsley, optional**

1. Preheat oven to 350°. In a large bowl, combine eggs, milk, cheese, saltines, carrots, onion, salt, garlic powder and pepper. Crumble beef over mixture and mix lightly but thoroughly. Shape into a loaf. Place in a greased 13x9-in. baking dish. Bake, uncovered, for 50 minutes.

2. For glaze, in a small saucepan, bring the brown sugar, ketchup and mustard to a boil. Reduce heat; simmer, uncovered, for 3-5 minutes or until heated through. Spoon over meat loaf.

3. Bake 10-15 minutes longer or until meat is no longer pink and a thermometer reads 160°. Drain; let stand for 10 minutes before slicing. If desired, top with minced fresh parsley.

1 PIECE: 266 cal., 12g fat (6g sat. fat), 100mg chol., 494mg sod., 18g carb. (12g sugars, 1g fiber), 20g pro.

MEAT LOAF SUCCESS TIPS
Follow these guidelines to master the classic comfort food.

- To ensure a tender loaf, avoid overmixing. Follow the recipe to combine the other loaf ingredients, then crumble the meat over the top and mix just until combined. Gently pat into a loaf shape.

- Experiment with different meat loaf toppings. Salsa, marinara, barbecue sauce or even jarred olive tapenade yield tasty results. Add toppings near the end of baking to ensure they do not burn.

- Get a jump on future meals by doubling the recipe and keeping the extra loaf in the freezer. Or portion this large loaf into 2 smaller ones. Then simply thaw in the refrigerator overnight and bake until done.

- For a classic Sunday dinner, serve the meat loaf with Mom's Potato Pancakes (p. 202) and Blue Cheese Kale Salad (p. 198).

GRILLED RIBEYE STEAKS

In the summer, I like to marinate steaks overnight,
then grill them for family and friends.
—Tim Hanchon, Muncie, IN

PREP: 10 MIN. + MARINATING • **GRILL:** 10 MIN. • **MAKES:** 6 SERVINGS

½ cup soy sauce	¼ tsp. ground ginger
½ cup sliced green onions	¼ tsp. pepper
¼ cup packed brown sugar	2½ lbs. beef ribeye steaks
2 garlic cloves, minced	

1. In a shallow dish, combine soy sauce, onions, brown sugar, garlic, ginger and pepper; add steaks and turn to coat. Refrigerate, covered, 8 hours or overnight.

2. Drain steaks, discarding marinade. Grill the steaks, covered, over medium heat until meat reaches desired doneness (for medium-rare, a thermometer should read 135°; medium, 140°; medium-well, 145°), 5-7 minutes on each side.

5 OZ. COOKED BEEF: 456 cal., 30g fat (12g sat. fat), 111mg chol., 1120mg sod., 8g carb. (8g sugars, 0 fiber), 36g pro.

RIBEYES WITH CHILI BUTTER

Combine 2 tsp. ground pepper and ¾ tsp. sugar; rub over steaks. Combine ⅔ cup butter, 2½ tsp. chili powder, 1¼ tsp. Dijon mustard and ⅛ tsp. cayenne pepper. Grill steaks as directed; top with chili butter.

BEEF COOKING METHODS AND CUTS

Tender cuts are best prepared with dry-heat cooking methods. For less-tender cuts, braising (cooking with moist heat) breaks down the fibers and yields tastier results.

Grilling or Broiling: Medium to high heat with a radiant heat source.

- Flank steak
- Flat iron steak
- T-bone/porterhouse
- Tri-tip steak

Pan-Searing: Quickly brown the meat on the stovetop over very high heat. Some cuts are seared, then finished in a hot oven.

- Ribeye steak
- Filet mignon
- New York strip steak
- Top sirloin or top round

Roasting: Brown the meat on high heat, then lower the temperature to cook more slowly.

- Rib roast
- Rump roast

Braising: Cook the meat in a small amount of liquid at low heat for a long time.

- Bottom round roast
- Brisket
- Chuck roast
- Eye of round
- Short ribs
- Top round roast

4 WAYS TO COOK HAMBURGERS

Shape 1⅓ lbs. ground beef into 4 patties, then chill. Sprinkle with ¾ tsp. salt and ¼ tsp. pepper just before cooking.

1) On the Grill: Preheat clean grill to medium heat. Cook burgers 5-7 minutes per side. If desired, add a slice of cheese to the burgers in the last minute of cooking; cover with the grill lid to help it melt.

2) On the Stove: Form patties with a doughnut-like hole in the middle. (Pan-fried burgers take a lot of direct heat; this promotes air-flow for more even cooking.) Heat skillet on medium-high to almost smoking; add a bit of butter to the pan and swirl to melt. Cook burgers 3-5 minutes on the first side, flip, then add a butter pat to each and continue cooking to desired temperature.

3) In the Oven: Preheat oven to 350°F. Place patties on a lightly greased (with butter or oil) baking sheet with plenty of room between them. Bake burgers 10 minutes, flip, then bake an additional 5-10 minutes.

4) In the Air Fryer: Preheat air fryer to 350°. Place patties in air-fryer basket, making sure they aren't touching; air-fry 5 minutes. Flip and cook an additional 3-5 minutes.

EASY GRILLED HAMBURGERS

These easy hamburgers come together in a snap.
—James Schend, Pleasant Prairie, WI

PREP: 20 MIN. • **GRILL:** 10 MIN.
MAKES: 4 SERVINGS

- 1⅓ lbs. ground beef
- ¾ tsp. salt
- ¼ tsp. pepper
- 4 hamburger buns, split and toasted
  Optional: Lettuce leaves, sliced tomato, sliced onion, bacon and mayonnaise

Shape ground beef into four ¾-in.-thick patties. Just before grilling, sprinkle with salt and pepper. Grill burgers, covered, over medium heat until a thermometer reads 160°, 5-7 minutes on each side. Top bun bottoms with the burgers. If desired, top with lettuce, tomato, onion, bacon and mayonnaise.

1 BURGER: 265 cal., 13g fat (5g sat. fat), 62mg chol., 495mg sod., 15g carb. (2g sugars, 1g fiber), 21g pro.

GREEN CHILE CHEESEBURGERS

Grill or broil 2 whole Anaheim or Hatch chiles until all sides are blistered and blackened, about 10 minutes. Immediately place peppers in a small bowl; let stand, covered, 20 minutes. Meanwhile, prepare burgers, adding a slice of sharp cheddar cheese to each in the last minute of cooking. Peel, seed and slice the peppers; place on burgers.

RESTAURANT-STYLE PRIME RIB

I have served this recipe to people visiting the U.S. from all over the world and to dear friends, family and neighbors. It is enjoyed and raved about by all. It makes an excellent main dish for a Christmas feast.
—Kelly Williams, Forked River, NJ

PREP: 10 MIN. • **COOK:** 2 HOURS + STANDING • **MAKES:** 8 SERVINGS

1 **bone-in beef rib roast (4 to 5 lbs.)**	2 **Tbsp. wasabi powder**
¼ **cup kosher salt**	2 **Tbsp. butter, softened**
2 **Tbsp. garlic powder**	1 **Tbsp. coarsely ground pepper**
2 **Tbsp. dried rosemary, crushed**	1 **tsp. herbes de Provence**

1. Preheat oven to 350°. Place roast, fat side up, on a rack in a foil-lined roasting pan. In a small bowl, mix kosher salt, garlic powder, rosemary, wasabi powder, butter, pepper and herbes de Provence; pat onto all sides of roast.

2. Roast 2-2½ hours or until meat reaches desired doneness (for medium-rare, a thermometer should read 135°; medium, 140°; medium-well 145°). Remove roast from oven; tent with foil. Let stand 15 minutes before carving.

5 OZ. COOKED BEEF: 311 cal., 18g fat (8g sat. fat), 8mg chol., 1624mg sod., 5g carb. (0 sugars, 1g fiber), 31g pro.

RAMEN STIR-FRY

This ramen stir-fry is unique and flavorful. The whole gang will enjoy this hearty, colorful meal-in-one recipe.
—Marlene McAllister, Portland, MI

TAKES: 30 MIN. • **MAKES:** 4 SERVINGS

1 **lb. ground beef**
1½ **cups sliced fresh carrots**
¾ **cup sliced onion**
1 **cup water**
1 **cup shredded cabbage**
1 **cup sliced fresh mushrooms**
1 **cup chopped green pepper**
3 **Tbsp. soy sauce**
1 **pkg. (3 oz.) beef ramen noodles**

1. In a large cast-iron or other heavy skillet, cook beef, carrots and onion over medium heat until the beef is no longer pink and the carrots are crisp-tender, 7-9 minutes, crumbling beef; drain.

2. Add water, cabbage, mushrooms, green pepper, soy sauce and contents of seasoning packet from noodles. Break noodles into small pieces; add to pan. Cover and cook until liquid is absorbed and noodles are tender, 8-10 minutes.

1½ CUPS: 379 cal., 18g fat (8g sat. fat), 86mg chol., 1202mg sod., 24g carb. (5g sugars, 3g fiber), 29g pro.

MAKE IT YOUR OWN

- To decrease sodium, use reduced-sodium soy sauce or tamari instead of regular, and use only half of the seasoning packet. These moves cut sodium by nearly 40%, saving 473mg per serving.

- Add your favorite ingredients with a variety of textures, such as chopped celery, canned water chestnuts or a sprinkling of sesame seeds or cashews.

REUBEN SANDWICHES

My mouth waters just thinking of these classic sandwiches.
I adapted the recipe from one my mother found several years ago.
—Kathy Jo Scott, Hemingford, NE

TAKES: 15 MIN. • **MAKES:** 4 SERVINGS

12 **oz. thinly sliced corned beef**
8 **slices light or dark rye bread**
1 **can (8 oz.) sauerkraut, rinsed and well drained**
½ **cup Thousand Island dressing**
4 **slices Swiss cheese**
   Butter

1. Arrange corned beef on 4 slices of bread. Layer each with a quarter of the sauerkraut, 2 Tbsp. of dressing and a slice of cheese. Top with the remaining bread slices. Butter outside of top piece of bread.

2. Place sandwich butter side down in a small skillet over medium heat; butter the outside of the new top piece of bread. Toast sandwiches until the bread is lightly browned on both sides and the cheese is melted.

1 SANDWICH: 547 cal., 31g fat (13g sat. fat), 106mg chol., 2346mg sod., 39g carb. (10g sugars, 5g fiber), 28g pro.

TRY BAKED MEATBALLS

Instead of frying, you can bake meatballs at 400° on a rack over a rimmed baking sheet until golden brown, about 20 minutes.

BEST SPAGHETTI & MEATBALLS

One evening, we had unexpected company. Since I had some of these meatballs left over in the freezer, I warmed them up as appetizers. Everyone raved! This classic recipe makes a big batch and is perfect for entertaining.
—Mary Lou Koskella, Prescott, AZ

PREP: 30 MIN. • **COOK:** 2 HOURS • **MAKES:** 16 SERVINGS

2	Tbsp. olive oil
1½	cups chopped onions
3	garlic cloves, minced
2	cans (12 oz. each) tomato paste
3	cups water
1	can (29 oz.) tomato sauce
⅓	cup minced fresh parsley
1	Tbsp. dried basil
2	tsp. salt
½	tsp. pepper

MEATBALLS

4	large eggs, lightly beaten
2	cups soft bread cubes (cut into ¼-in. pieces)
1½	cups 2% milk
1	cup grated Parmesan cheese
3	garlic cloves, minced
2	tsp. salt
½	tsp. pepper
3	lbs. ground beef
2	Tbsp. canola oil
2	lbs. spaghetti, cooked

1. In a Dutch oven, heat olive oil over medium heat. Add onions; saute until softened. Add garlic; cook 1 minute longer. Stir in tomato paste; cook 3-5 minutes. Add next 6 ingredients. Bring to a boil. Reduce heat; simmer, covered, for 50 minutes.

2. Combine the first 7 meatball ingredients. Add beef; mix lightly but thoroughly. Shape into 1½-in. balls.

3. In a large skillet, heat canola oil over medium heat. Add meatballs; brown in batches until no longer pink. Drain. Add to sauce; bring to a boil. Reduce heat; simmer, covered, until flavors are blended, about 1 hour, stirring occasionally. Serve with hot cooked spaghetti.

½ CUP SAUCE WITH 4 MEATBALLS AND 1¼ CUPS SPAGHETTI: 519 cal., 18g fat (6g sat. fat), 106mg chol., 1043mg sod., 59g carb. (8g sugars, 4g fiber), 30g pro.

FREEZER DIRECTIONS

Simmer the meatballs and sauce as directed. Cool, then place in freezer containers. Make sure the meatballs are covered with sauce so they don't dry out. Freeze. To use, thaw overnight in the refrigerator. Place meatballs and sauce in a Dutch oven over medium heat; cook, stirring occasionally, until heated through.

ULTIMATE POT ROAST

Pot roasts are the ultimate comfort food. When a juicy pot roast simmers in garlic, onions and veggies, everyone comes running to ask, "When can we eat?" The answer? "Just wait—it will be worth it!"
—Nick Iverson, Denver, CO

PREP: 55 MIN. • **BAKE:** 2 HOURS • **MAKES:** 8 SERVINGS

- 1 boneless beef chuck-eye or other chuck roast (3 to 4 lbs.)
- 2 tsp. pepper
- 2 tsp. salt, divided
- 2 Tbsp. canola oil
- 2 medium onions, cut into 1-in. pieces
- 2 celery ribs, chopped
- 3 garlic cloves, minced
- 1 Tbsp. tomato paste
- 1 Tbsp. minced fresh thyme or 1 tsp. dried thyme
- 2 bay leaves
- 1 cup dry red wine or reduced-sodium beef broth
- 2 cups reduced-sodium beef broth
- 1 lb. small red potatoes, quartered
- 4 medium parsnips, peeled and cut into 2-in. pieces
- 6 medium carrots, cut into 2-in. pieces
- 1 Tbsp. red wine vinegar
- 2 Tbsp. minced fresh parsley Salt and pepper to taste

1. Preheat oven to 325°. Pat roast dry with a paper towel; tie at 2-in. intervals with kitchen string for even cooking. Sprinkle roast with pepper and 1½ tsp. salt. In a Dutch oven, heat oil over medium-high heat. Brown roast on all sides. Remove from pot.

2. Add onions, celery and ½ tsp. salt to the same pot; cook and stir over medium heat 8-10 minutes or until the onions are browned. Add garlic, tomato paste, thyme and bay leaves; cook and stir 1 minute longer.

3. Add wine, stirring to loosen browned bits from pot; stir in broth. Return roast to pot. Arrange potatoes, parsnips and carrots around roast; bring to a boil. Bake, covered, until meat is fork-tender, 2-2½ hours.

4. Remove roast and vegetables from pot; keep warm. Discard bay leaves; skim fat from cooking juices. On stovetop, bring juices to a boil; cook until liquid is reduced by half (about 1½ cups), 10-12 minutes. Stir in vinegar and parsley; season with salt and pepper to taste.

5. Remove string from roast. Serve with vegetables and sauce.

3 OZ. COOKED BEEF WITH 1 CUP VEGETABLES AND 3 TBSP. SAUCE:
459 cal., 20g fat (7g sat. fat), 112mg chol., 824mg sod., 32g carb. (8g sugars, 6g fiber), 37g pro.

TYING A ROAST

Step 1: Pat roast dry. Slip a long piece of kitchen string under the roast and tie it tightly.

Step 2: Continue tying at 2-in. intervals, making roast as compact as possible.

Step 3: Trim loose ends of string; proceed with the recipe.

POT ROAST POINTERS

Chuck is the ideal cut for this type of low-and-slow braising because it has plenty of marbling and collagen. This translates to tenderness and flavor! Brisket is an excellent choice too.

Lean cuts like rump and round roasts will work but will not be nearly as moist and fall-apart tender.

It can be tempting to skip the searing step, but browning the outside of a roast before cooking it helps to build layers of flavor. Those browned bits in the pan make a flavorful gravy.

SIRLOIN TIP
ROAST POINTERS

Be sure to slice tip roast and other beef cuts against the grain. This allows for a more tender meat. You can easily find the grain by looking on the outside to see which way the muscle fibers run. Then slice the meat across the fibers, in the opposite direction.

Any leftover meat will make a killer roast beef sandwich the next day. Or you can use leftovers in ramen or chimichangas.

THE BEST GRILLED SIRLOIN TIP ROAST

If you're looking for a flavorful cut of meat that's still pretty lean, give this sirloin tip roast recipe a try. I like to cook it slowly over indirect heat, mopping it frequently with red wine sauce.
—James Schend, Pleasant Prairie, WI

PREP: 40 MIN. + CHILLING • **GRILL:** 1½ HOURS + STANDING • **MAKES:** 6 SERVINGS

1 beef sirloin tip roast or beef tri-tip roast (2 to 3 lbs.)	6 fresh thyme sprigs
1 Tbsp. kosher salt	1 garlic cloves, crushed
2 tsp. dried thyme	½ tsp. whole peppercorns
2 tsp. garlic powder	3 whole cloves
1 tsp. coarsely ground pepper	
1 small onion, chopped	HORSERADISH-THYME BUTTER (OPTIONAL)
2 Tbsp. olive oil, divided	6 Tbsp. softened butter
1 bottle (750 ml) dry red wine	2 Tbsp. prepared horseradish
	3 Tbsp. fresh thyme leaves

1. Sprinkle roast with salt, thyme, garlic powder and ground pepper. Refrigerate, covered, at least 8 hours or up to 24 hours. Meanwhile, in a saucepan, saute onion in 1 Tbsp. oil until tender, about 5 minutes. Add wine, thyme, garlic, peppercorns and cloves. Simmer until reduced to ¾ cup. Cool; strain, discarding solids, and refrigerate.

2. Remove roast from the refrigerator 1 hour before grilling. Prepare grill for indirect heat, using a drip pan. Add wood chips according to manufacturer's directions.

3. Pat roast dry with paper towels. Brush with remaining 1 Tbsp. oil; place over drip pan. Grill, covered, over medium-low indirect heat, brushing with mop sauce every 20 minutes, until meat reaches desired doneness (for medium-rare, a thermometer should read 135°; medium, 140°; medium-well, 145°), 1½-2 hours. Let roast stand for 15 minutes before slicing.

4. If desired, in a small bowl, stir together butter, horseradish and thyme. Serve on top of roast.

4 OZ. COOKED BEEF: 262 cal., 13g fat (4g sat. fat), 91mg chol., 1027mg sod., 3g carb. (1g sugars, 1g fiber), 32g pro.

CAST-IRON SKILLET STEAK

If you've never cooked steak at home before, it can be a little intimidating. That's why I came up with this simple steak recipe that's so easy, you could make it any day of the week.
—James Schend, Pleasant Prairie, WI

PREP: 5 MIN. + STANDING • **COOK:** 5 MIN. • **MAKES:** 2 SERVINGS

3 tsp. kosher salt, divided	**1** beef New York strip or ribeye steak (1 lb.), 1 in. thick

1. Remove steak from refrigerator and sprinkle with 2 tsp. salt; let stand 45-60 minutes.

2. Preheat a cast-iron skillet over high heat until extremely hot, 4-5 minutes. Sprinkle remaining 1 tsp. salt in bottom of skillet; pat beef dry with paper towels. Place steak in skillet and cook until easily moved, 1-2 minutes; flip, placing steak in a different section of the skillet. Cook 30 seconds and then begin moving steak, occasionally pressing slightly to ensure even contact with skillet.

3. Continue turning and flipping until steak is cooked to desired degree of doneness (for medium-rare, a thermometer should read 135°; medium, 140°; medium-well, 145°), 1-2 minutes.

6 OZ. COOKED BEEF: 494 cal., 36g fat (15g sat. fat), 134mg chol., 2983mg sod., 0 carb. (0 sugars, 0 fiber), 40g pro.

SKILLET STEAK TIPS

For a juicy, tender steak, choose 1 with a plenty of marbling. It may be more expensive, but the result will be worth it.

For a flavor burst, baste your steak with butter near the end of cooking. Be sure to turn down the heat so the butter doesn't burn. Consider 1 of the flavored butters on p. 106.

If you don't have cast iron, you can cook the steak in another type of skillet. However, it won't develop the amazing crust an ultra-hot cast-iron pan delivers. Some materials, such as nonstick, are not safe to heat to very high temperatures.

CHECK OUT HOW EASY THIS IS

Just hover your camera here.

TRADITIONAL BOILED DINNER

Corned beef is a frequent treat in our family. We love the savory flavor the vegetables pick up from simmering with the pickling spices.
—Joy Strasser, Mukwonago, WI

PREP: 10 MIN. • **COOK:** 2½ HOURS • **MAKES:** 6 SERVINGS

- 1 **corned beef brisket with spice packet (3 lbs.)**
- 1 **tsp. whole black peppercorns**
- 2 **bay leaves**
- 2 **medium potatoes, peeled and quartered**
- 3 **medium carrots, quartered**
- 1 **medium onion, cut into 6 wedges**
- 1 **small head green cabbage, cut into 6 wedges**
- **Optional: Prepared horseradish or mustard**

1. Place the brisket and the contents of the spice packet in a Dutch oven. Add peppercorns, bay leaves and enough water to cover; bring to a boil. Reduce heat; simmer, covered, for 2 hours or until meat is almost tender.

2. Add the potatoes, carrots and onion; bring to a boil. Reduce heat; simmer, covered, for 10 minutes. Add cabbage; simmer, covered, for 15-20 minutes or until meat and vegetables are tender. Discard bay leaves and peppercorns. Thinly slice meat; serve with vegetables and, if desired, horseradish or mustard.

8 OZ. COOKED BEEF WITH VEGETABLES: 558 cal., 34g fat (11g sat. fat), 122mg chol., 2797mg sod., 25g carb. (8g sugars, 5g fiber), 37g pro.

BOILED DINNER Q&A

Can you use a different kind of meat? A beef roast and ham are both great substitutes. The beef roast has a rich flavor like corned beef and will cook for a similar timeframe. Ham will have a sweeter flavor and will heat up fast if you're short on time.

Can you make this in the slow cooker? Absolutely! Place vegetables in the slow cooker, add brisket and enough water to cover meat. Cook, covered, on low for 8-9 hours or until fork-tender and the internal temperature reaches 145°. Add the cabbage on top of the brisket during the last 2 hours of cooking.

How do you store leftovers? Use shallow containers so the food cools quickly. Refrigerate up to 3 days or freeze for up to 6 months. You can use leftover corned beef to make delicious Reuben Sandwiches (p. 156).

HERB & CHEESE-STUFFED BURGERS

Tired of the same old ground beef burgers? This quick-fix alternative, with its creamy cheese filling, will wake up your taste buds.
—Sherri Cox, Lucasville, OH

TAKES: 30 MIN. • **MAKES:** 4 SERVINGS

¼ cup shredded cheddar cheese	½ tsp. salt
2 Tbsp. cream cheese, softened	½ tsp. dried rosemary, crushed
2 Tbsp. minced fresh parsley	¼ tsp. dried sage leaves
3 tsp. Dijon mustard, divided	1 lb. lean ground beef (90% lean)
2 green onions, thinly sliced	4 hamburger buns, split
3 Tbsp. dry bread crumbs	Optional toppings: Lettuce leaves and tomato slices
2 Tbsp. ketchup	

1. In a small bowl, mix cheddar cheese, cream cheese, parsley and 1 tsp. mustard. In another bowl, mix green onions, bread crumbs, ketchup, seasonings and remaining mustard. Add beef; mix lightly but thoroughly.

2. Shape beef mixture into 8 thin patties. Spoon cheese mixture onto the center of each of 4 patties; top with the remaining patties, pressing edges firmly to seal.

3. Grill burgers, covered, over medium heat or broil 4 in. from heat until a thermometer reads 160°, 4-5 minutes on each side. Serve on buns with toppings as desired.

1 BURGER: 383 cal., 16g fat (7g sat. fat), 86mg chol., 861mg sod., 29g carb. (5g sugars, 1g fiber), 29g pro.

AIR-FRIED VARIATION

Preheat air fryer to 375°. Working in batches if necessary, place burgers in a single layer on the tray in the air-fryer basket. Cook for 8 minutes. Flip; cook until a thermometer inserted in burger reads 160°, 6-8 minutes longer. Serve burgers on buns with toppings as desired.

HOW TO STUFF BURGERS

Step 1: Shape mixture into 8 thin patties.

Step 2: Top half of burgers with desired fillings.

Step 3: Enclose with remaining burgers. Firmly press edges to ensure a good seal.

GET GLOBAL WITH THESE VARIATIONS

- **Capri:** Give your burger an Italian twist by combining ripe tomatoes, a bit of basil and fresh mozzarella for the filling.

- **Mexicali:** Pack a little Tex-Mex-style heat by using fresh jalapeno and pepper jack cheese.

- **Mykonos:** Make a Greek-flavored burger by filling it with chopped baby spinach and crumbled feta cheese.

PORK, LAMB & MORE

From crown roast and lamb chops to quick Chinese fried rice and restaurant-inspired gyro salad, versatile recipes for every occasion can be found here. Discover dry and wet rubs, the best pulled pork buns, savory pies and more.

DIJON-RUBBED PORK WITH RHUBARB SAUCE

This moist and tender pork loin roast is served with a rhubarb sauce that's just delicious! It's perfect for company and makes an extra-special weeknight meal.
—Marilyn Rodriguez, Sparks, NV

PREP: 15 MIN. • **BAKE:** 1 HOUR + STANDING
MAKES: 12 SERVINGS (1½ CUPS SAUCE)

1 **boneless pork loin roast (3 lbs.)**
¼ **cup Dijon mustard**
6 **garlic cloves, minced**
1 **Tbsp. minced fresh rosemary or 1 tsp. dried rosemary, crushed**
¾ **tsp. salt**
½ **tsp. pepper**

SAUCE
3 **cups sliced fresh or frozen rhubarb**
⅓ **cup orange juice**
⅓ **cup sugar**
1 **Tbsp. cider vinegar**

1. Score the surface of the pork, making diamond shapes ¼ in. deep. In a small bowl, combine the mustard, garlic, rosemary, salt and pepper; rub over pork.

2. Coat a roasting pan and rack with cooking spray; place pork on rack in pan. Bake, uncovered, at 350° for 1 hour or until a thermometer reads 145°. Let stand for 10 minutes before slicing.

3. Meanwhile, in a small saucepan, bring the sauce ingredients to a boil. Reduce heat; cover and simmer for 8-12 minutes or until rhubarb is tender. Serve warm, with pork.

3 OZ. COOKED PORK WITH 2 TBSP. SAUCE: 181 cal., 6g fat (2g sat. fat), 56mg chol., 308mg sod., 9g carb. (7g sugars, 1g fiber), 23g pro.
DIABETIC EXCHANGES: 3 lean meat, ½ starch.

TEST KITCHEN TIP

To help give pork loin a uniform shape and ensure even cooking, cinch it with several loops of butcher's twine before roasting.

RHUBARB 101
Here are some fun facts on the sweet-tart treat.

What is rhubarb? Rhubarb is a perennial that grows well in cool climates. The stalks are edible, but it's sometimes planted as an ornamental plant because of its beautiful, vibrant red stalks and broad green leaves. Tasted plain, rhubarb is intensely tart. But add some sugar and the vegetable becomes quite enjoyable.

When is rhubarb in season? Rhubarb grows best in weather below 75°, so it's widely available in spring. You'll find it in most areas beginning in April or May, although some regions have rhubarb all summer.

How do I choose rhubarb? Look for firm, shiny stalks without any blemishes. If attached, the leaves should look fresh and firm. Dark red rhubarb is sweeter and more flavorful, but green stalks are edible too.

HOW TO MINCE GARLIC BY HAND

Step 1: Make 3-4 horizontal cuts lengthwise in garlic clove, making sure not to cut all the way through the base.

Step 2: Next, make 3-4 vertical lengthwise cuts, slicing all the way through clove.

Step 3: Finish by cutting garlic crosswise, all the way through the clove, resulting in uniform-sized pieces of garlic.

HUNGARIAN TREASURE (SZEKELY GULYAS)

This combination of pork, sauerkraut, sour cream and paprika is heavenly served on buttery egg noodles with or without poppy seeds. Here's to comfort food!
—*Taste of Home* Test Kitchen

PREP: 25 MIN. • **COOK:** 3 HOURS • **MAKES:** 6 SERVINGS

1½ lbs. pork tenderloin, cubed
¼ tsp. salt
¼ tsp. pepper
1 Tbsp. olive oil
2 Tbsp. butter
1 large onion, chopped
6 garlic cloves, minced
½ tsp. smoked paprika
2 pkg. (1 lb. each) sauerkraut, rinsed and well drained
½ cup water
1½ cups sour cream
½ tsp. poppy seeds
    Hot cooked buttered egg noodles

1. Sprinkle pork with salt and pepper. In a large skillet, heat oil over medium-high heat; brown meat. Transfer meat to a 4- or 5-qt. slow cooker. In the same skillet, melt butter over medium-high heat. Add onion; cook and stir until tender, 6-8 minutes. Add garlic and paprika; cook 1 minute longer. Pour over meat. Add sauerkraut and water.

2. Cook, covered, on low until pork is tender, 3-4 hours. Stir in sour cream; sprinkle with poppy seeds. Serve with noodles.

1⅓ CUPS: 369 cal., 25g fat (12g sat. fat), 79mg chol., 1181mg sod., 12g carb. (6g sugars, 5g fiber), 26g pro.

ORIGIN OF SZEKELY GULYAS

It may sound exotic, but this dish is more familiar than you might think. The stew's name comes from the Szekely people, a large group of ethnic Hungarians living in present-day Romania. Gulyas is the same as what Americans call goulash—a varied and wonderful family of paprika-seasoned, stewlike comfort foods. This version from Szekely always includes sauerkraut, onions and sour cream.

DRY-RUB PORK CHOPS OVER CANNELLINI BEANS & GREENS

My family was not a huge fan of pork until I tried this recipe. Feel free to incorporate your favorite herbs into the dry rub. You can use the rub on boneless skinless chicken breast or other meats too.
—Michael Cirlincione, Stockton, NJ

PREP: 20 MIN. • **COOK:** 25 MIN. • **MAKES:** 4 SERVINGS

1 Tbsp. olive oil
1 medium onion, chopped
2 garlic cloves, minced
1 can (15 oz.) cannellini beans, rinsed and drained
1 cup water-packed artichoke hearts, drained and chopped
¾ cup pitted Greek olives, chopped
¼ cup dry white wine or chicken broth
¼ cup chicken broth
¼ tsp. salt
¼ tsp. smoked paprika
¼ tsp. pepper
4 bone-in pork loin chops (8 oz. each)
2 tsp. Greek seasoning or seasoning of your choice
5 oz. fresh baby spinach (about 6 cups)

1. In a large skillet, heat oil over medium-high heat. Add onion; cook and stir until tender 4-5 minutes. Add garlic; cook 1 minute longer. Stir in beans, artichokes, olives, wine, broth, salt, paprika and pepper. Bring to a boil; reduce heat. Simmer until liquid is almost evaporated, 12-15 minutes.

2. Meanwhile, sprinkle chops with Greek seasoning. Grill pork chops over medium heat until a thermometer reads 145°, 6-8 minutes on each side. Let stand 5 minutes before serving.

3. Stir spinach into bean mixture; cook and stir until wilted, 2-3 minutes. Serve with pork.

1 SERVING: 530 cal., 29g fat (8g sat. fat), 111mg chol., 1345mg sod., 22g carb. (1g sugars, 6g fiber), 42g pro.

SEASON IT YOUR WAY

Spice up your chops, ribs and more—literally!—with these dry and wet rubs. Stir together the ingredients, then slather.

- **All-American Rub:** ¼ cup packed brown sugar, 1 Tbsp. dried minced onion, 1½ tsp. garlic powder, 1½ tsp. ground mustard, ¼ tsp. cayenne, dash nutmeg

- **Spicy Rib Rub:** 3 Tbsp. paprika, 2 Tbsp.+ 1 tsp. salt, 2 Tbsp.+ 1 tsp. garlic powder, 2 Tbsp. cayenne pepper, 4 tsp. onion powder, 4 tsp. dried oregano, 4 tsp. dried thyme and 4 tsp. pepper

- **Basil Rub:** ¼ cup packed brown sugar, 1½ tsp. dried basil, ½ tsp. salt, ½ tsp. chili powder and 1 Tbsp. canola oil

- **Herbed Rub:** 1 tsp. salt-free garlic seasoning blend, ½ tsp. dried basil, ½ tsp. dried oregano, ½ tsp. dried parsley flakes, ¼ tsp. salt, ¼ tsp. garlic powder and ¼ tsp. crushed dried rosemary

SUGAR-GLAZED HAM TIPS

Do you add water to bake a ham? It depends! Always follow the directions in the recipe. Some call to add an inch of water to the bottom of the roasting pan. You then cover the ham tightly with foil to create steam and moisture. For this recipe, you don't need to add water.

Do you glaze ham before or after cooking? It's best to glaze ham during the last 15 to 30 minutes of cooking. If you glaze ham too early, the sugar in the glaze could scorch or harden.

How do you moisten a dry ham? Glazing can help moisten a dry ham. You can also pour some broth or water over a dry ham, cover it tightly and bake the ham, basting occasionally with the cooking liquids. This is also an effective way to moisten and enjoy any leftover ham.

HOW TO PREP, GLAZE & CARVE A HAM

Step 1: With sharp knife, score ham with ¼-in.-deep cuts in a diamond pattern. This will allow the glaze to penetrate into the ham. Add cloves if desired.

Step 2: Carefully apply glaze near the end of bake time.

Step 3: Place ham, flat side down, on cutting board. Securing meat with a fork, carve along the bone with a sharp knife to remove the boneless section.

Step 4: Slice the boneless section vertically. Set the slices on a serving plate, tenting with foil to keep warm.

Step 5: With the remaining bone-in portion, insert fork into the meat directly next to the bone. Make horizontal cuts until you reach the bone.

Step 6: Finally, slice bone-in portion vertically along the bone. This cuts off the horizontal slices, which fall neatly onto the board. Transfer them to the serving plate and serve.

SUGAR-GLAZED HAM

This old-fashioned sugar glaze gives your ham a pretty golden-brown coating just like Grandma used to make. The mustard and vinegar complement the brown sugar and add tangy flavor. Be prepared to serve seconds!
—Carol Strong Battle, Heathsville, VA

PREP: 5 MIN. • **BAKE:** 1¾ HOURS
MAKES: 14 SERVINGS

- 1 **fully cooked bone-in ham (5 to 7 lbs.)**
- 1 **cup packed brown sugar**
- 2 **tsp. prepared mustard**
- 1 **to 2 Tbsp. cider vinegar**

1. Preheat oven to 325°. Place ham on a rack in a shallow roasting pan. Using a sharp knife, score surface of ham with ¼-in.-deep cuts in a diamond pattern. Cover and bake until a thermometer reads 130°, 1½-2 hours.

2. Meanwhile, in a small bowl, combine brown sugar, mustard and enough vinegar to make a thick paste. Remove ham from oven. Spread sugar mixture over ham. Bake, uncovered, until a thermometer reads 140°, 15-30 minutes longer.

4 OZ. HAM: 284 cal., 16g fat (6g sat. fat), 57mg chol., 1110mg sod., 15g carb. (15g sugars, 0 fiber), 20g pro.

PORK BANH MI WRAPS

Crunchy veggies and Asian flavors make this a fantastic wrap for summer. You can substitute a baguette for the wrap, or switch up the meat for five-spice chicken or spicy beef. Even lemongrass shrimp would be delicious!
—Nicole Hood, Leesville, LA

TAKES: 30 MIN. • **MAKES:** 4 SERVINGS

4 boneless pork loin chops (4 oz. each)	2 Tbsp. rice vinegar
¼ tsp. pepper	4 bread wraps (9 in.)
1 Tbsp. olive oil	¼ cup reduced-fat mayonnaise
½ cup sweet chili sauce, divided	1 small cucumber, peeled and sliced into 3-in. strips
2 Tbsp. reduced-sodium soy sauce	¼ cup chopped fresh cilantro
1¼ cups shredded lettuce	2 green onions, chopped
1 medium carrot, peeled and shredded	½ jalapeno pepper, seeded and thinly sliced
	Sriracha chili sauce

1. Sprinkle pork chops with pepper. In a large cast-iron or other heavy skillet, heat oil over medium heat. Add chops; cook until a thermometer reads 145°, 2-3 minutes on each side. Combine ¼ cup sweet chili sauce with soy sauce; pour over chops. Reduce heat to medium-low; cook and stir until sauce is slightly thickened, 2-3 minutes. Remove from heat.

2. Combine lettuce and carrot with rice vinegar; set aside. When pork is cool enough to handle, slice into 2-in.-long strips; return to skillet to coat with sauce. Toast bread wraps lightly, then spread with mayonnaise.

3. Spoon pork evenly over wraps. Cover with lettuce mixture, cucumber, cilantro, green onions and jalapeno. Top with remaining sweet chili sauce. Fold wraps over filling and serve immediately with Sriracha sauce.

1 FILLED WRAP: 471 cal., 18g fat (4g sat. fat), 60mg chol., 1344mg sod., 54g carb. (21g sugars, 7g fiber), 26g pro.

HOW TO QUICK-PICKLE VEGGIES

A pickled daikon and carrot blend, known as *do chua*, is a Vietnamese condiment traditionally served with banh mi. You can whip up your own *do chua* to serve with the pork mixture instead of shredded lettuce and carrot.

Peel and julienne 1 medium daikon radish, or thinly slice ¾ lb. Easter egg or regular radishes. Julienne 2 carrots; seed and thinly slice 2 jalapenos. Place in a large bowl.

In a small saucepan, combine ¾ cup water, ¾ cup white vinegar, ⅓ cup sugar and ¾ tsp. salt. Bring to a boil; simmer until sugar dissolves. Pour mixture over vegetables, ensuring vegetables are submerged; cool. Refrigerate, covered, at least 1 hour before serving. Store in the refrigerator for up to 2 weeks, stirring pickles occasionally.

CUSTOMIZE THE HEAT LEVEL

Up to 80% of the capsaicin (the compound that gives peppers their heat) is in the seeds and the membranes. To reduce the heat in the dish, cut the peppers in half and use a spoon to scrape out the seeds and membranes. If you like spicy foods, add a few seeds to the dish instead of discarding them. When handling hot peppers—especially if you have sensitive skin—wear rubber gloves and avoid touching your face.

ABOUT TZATZIKI

The dressing recipe is a riff on Greek tzatziki sauce, a blend of yogurt, cucumber, garlic, and often lemon and dill. You can make your own quick version of tzatziki sauce with plain yogurt or sour cream, cucumber, and the herbs and seasonings you prefer.

GYRO SALAD WITH TZATZIKI DRESSING

If you're fond of gyros, you'll enjoy this garden-fresh salad showcasing ground lamb, crumbled feta cheese, Greek olives, tomatoes and a creamy cucumber dressing.
—*Taste of Home* Test Kitchen

TAKES: 30 MIN. • **MAKES:** 6 SERVINGS

DRESSING
- 1 **cucumber, peeled and coarsely shredded**
- ½ **tsp. salt**
- ½ **cup sour cream**
- ¾ **cup plain yogurt**
- 2 **Tbsp. white vinegar**
- 1 **garlic clove, minced**
- ½ **tsp. dill weed**
- ¼ **tsp. cracked black pepper**

SALAD
- ½ **lb. ground lamb or ground beef**
- 1 **small onion, chopped**
- 1 **tsp. Greek seasoning or oregano leaves**
- 8 **cups mixed salad greens**
- 2 **tomatoes, chopped**
- 1 **pkg. (4 oz.) crumbled feta cheese**
- ½ **cup pitted Greek olives, drained**
  Toasted pita bread wedges

1. In a large bowl, sprinkle cucumber with salt; mix well. Let stand 5 minutes. Drain. Stir in the remaining dressing ingredients. Cover and refrigerate.

2. In a large skillet over medium-high heat, cook lamb, onion and Greek seasoning until lamb is no longer pink, stirring to break the meat into crumbles; drain.

3. Arrange salad mix on a large serving platter; top with tomatoes, cheese, olives and lamb. Spoon dressing over salad. Serve immediately with toasted pita wedges.

1 SERVING: 236 cal., 16g fat (7g sat. fat), 43mg chol., 807mg sod., 10g carb. (4g sugars, 3g fiber), 14g pro.

GYRO SALAD TIPS

- **Is gyro salad healthy?** Gyro salad is a good way to get in more vegetables, and it's better for you than many gyros—but it's a little high in saturated fat and sodium to be considered healthy. To make it healthier, dial back the feta cheese and use ground lamb or beef that's at least 90% lean. Or choose lean ground chicken or turkey.

- **What are some variations of gyro salad?** To make this salad heartier, grill or toast some pita breads, cut into wedges, and toss them right into the mix. Or add fresh mint leaves for a refreshing, summer-perfect touch.

- **How do you store gyro salad with tzatziki dressing?** Keep the dressing separate whenever possible so it doesn't wilt your salad greens. Cover and refrigerate the leftovers for up to 3 days.

IRISH STEW PIE

The only thing more comforting than a hearty bowl of Irish stew is when it's baked into a pie! The flavors blend well with lamb, but you can use cuts of beef instead if you wish.
—Nicolas Hortense, Perth, Australia

PREP: 1 HOUR • **BAKE:** 35 MIN. + STANDING • **MAKES:** 6 SERVINGS

- ½ cup plus 1 Tbsp. all-purpose flour, divided
- ¾ tsp. salt, divided
- ¾ tsp. pepper, divided
- 1 lb. boneless lamb shoulder roast, cubed
- 2 Tbsp. canola oil
- 2 medium carrots, finely chopped
- 1 medium onion, halved and sliced
- 1¼ cups beef stock
- 2 medium Yukon Gold potatoes, peeled and cubed
- 1 fresh thyme sprig
- 1 bay leaf
- 1 tsp. Worcestershire sauce
- 1 tsp. tomato paste
- 3 Tbsp. chopped fresh mint
- 1 large egg yolk
- 2 Tbsp. heavy whipping cream
- 1 pkg. (17.3 oz.) frozen puff pastry, thawed

1. Preheat oven to 350°. In a shallow bowl, mix ½ cup flour, ½ tsp. salt and ½ tsp. pepper. Add lamb, a few pieces at a time, and toss to coat; shake off excess. In a Dutch oven, heat oil over medium-high heat. Brown lamb in batches. Remove from pan. Add carrots and onion to same pan; cook and stir until crisp-tender, 6-8 minutes. Stir in remaining 1 Tbsp. flour until blended; gradually whisk in stock. Bring to a boil, stirring to loosen browned bits from pan.

2. Add potatoes, thyme, bay leaf, Worcestershire sauce, tomato paste, the remaining ¼ tsp. salt and ¼ tsp. pepper, and lamb; return to a boil. Reduce heat. Simmer, uncovered, until sauce is thickened and lamb is tender, 25-30 minutes. Discard thyme sprig and bay leaf. Stir in mint. Transfer to a greased 9-in. deep-dish pie plate. Whisk egg yolk and cream; brush around edge of pie plate to help pastry adhere.

3. On a lightly floured surface, unfold 1 sheet puff pastry; top with remaining sheet. Roll to fit over pie plate. Carefully place over filling; trim to fit. Using a fork, press crust firmly onto rim of pie plate to seal edge. Brush with remaining egg mixture; cut slits in top. Place on a rimmed baking sheet. Bake until golden brown, 35-40 minutes. Let stand 10 minutes before serving.

1 SERVING: 731 cal., 40g fat (11g sat. fat), 75mg chol., 608mg sod., 71g carb. (4g sugars, 8g fiber), 24g pro.

MAKE IT A SHEPHERD'S PIE

Another savory pie option popular in the U.K. is shepherd's pie.

Rather than a pastry crust, shepherd's pie is topped with hot mashed potatoes, then baked or broiled until golden brown. Consider Garlic Mashed Red Potatoes (p. 213) as a topper for this recipe.

Shepherd's pie is often prepared with thrifty cooked ground beef or lamb rather than stew meat. To use it, stir 1 lb. of ground meat, cooked and drained, into the prepared vegetable mixture before transferring to the pie plate. Omit mint if desired.

VIEW 44
MORE IRISH
CLASSICS
Just hover your
camera here.

CLASSIC CHOP FRILLS

Those little paper chef hats have a name: chop frills. They're used to conceal the ends of rib bones on a crown roast or lamb chops, and on poultry drumsticks. Your butcher might provide chop frills when you order a crown roast, or you can find them in kitchen-supply stores.

Chop frills date back to the 1800s, when they were used primarily to hide the "unsightly" ends of the bones. Some people like the classic look.

CORNBREAD-STUFFED CROWN ROAST

My mother always made this elegant entree for company dinners and special family celebrations.
—Dorothy Swanson, St. Louis, MO

PREP: 20 MIN. • **BAKE:** 3 HOURS + STANDING • **MAKES:** 12 SERVINGS

1   pork crown roast (about 7 lbs. and 12 ribs)
½   tsp. pepper, divided
1   cup butter, cubed
1   cup chopped celery
1   cup chopped onion
6   cups crushed cornbread stuffing
2   cups frozen corn, thawed
2   jars (4½ oz. each) sliced mushrooms, undrained
1   tsp. salt
1   tsp. poultry seasoning

1. Preheat oven to 350°. Place the roast on a rack in a large shallow roasting pan. Sprinkle with ¼ tsp. pepper. Cover rib ends with foil. Bake, uncovered, for 1½ hours.

2. Melt butter in a Dutch oven over medium heat. Cook and stir celery and onion until tender, 3-5 minutes. Stir in the stuffing, corn, mushrooms, salt, poultry seasoning and remaining pepper. Carefully spoon 1-3 cups into center of roast. Place remaining stuffing in a greased 2-qt. baking dish. Refrigerate until ready to use.

3. Bake roast until a thermometer inserted in stuffing reads 140°, about 1 hour. Cover and bake the extra stuffing until browned, 30-40 minutes. Transfer to a serving platter. Let stand for 15 minutes. Remove foil. Cut between ribs to serve.

1 SERVING: 545 cal., 30g fat (15g sat. fat), 124mg chol., 826mg sod., 30g carb. (3g sugars, 3g fiber), 38g pro.

ORDERING CROWN ROAST

A crown roast is a meat cut originating from the rib section of the loin. Two racks of ribs are combined in a circle and roasted, ribs up, in a shape resembling a crown. The crown's center is often filled with stuffing.

Order your crown roast at least a week before you plan to serve it, since it's a specialty cut. An experienced butcher can help select one that you're less likely to under- or overcook. Be specific about the number of servings you need, since roasts can vary in size (and chop count) depending on how they're trimmed and prepped.

HOISIN SHREDDED PORK SANDWICHES

On cool-weather weeknights, the slow cooker is our friend. The plums might surprise in these juicy pork sandwiches, but they add a little sweetness and make the meat extra tender.
—Holly Battiste, Barrington, NJ

PREP: 30 MIN. • **COOK:** 6 HOURS • **MAKES:** 10 SERVINGS

- 1 can (15 oz.) plums, drained and pitted
- 1 Tbsp. Sriracha chili sauce
- 1 Tbsp. hoisin sauce
- 1 Tbsp. reduced-sodium soy sauce
- 1 Tbsp. rice vinegar
- 1 Tbsp. honey
- 2 garlic cloves, minced
- 1 tsp. pepper
- 1 tsp. sesame oil
- ½ tsp. ground ginger
- ¼ tsp. salt
- 2 Tbsp. canola oil
- 1 boneless pork shoulder butt roast (3 lbs.)
- 4 medium carrots, finely chopped
- 10 ciabatta rolls, split
      Shredded napa or other cabbage

1. Mix first 11 ingredients. In a large skillet, heat oil over medium-high heat. Brown roast on all sides.

2. Place carrots in a 4- or 5-qt. slow cooker. Add roast; pour plum mixture over top. Cook, covered, on low until pork is tender, 6-8 hours.

3. Remove pork; shred with 2 forks. Skim fat from carrot mixture; stir in pork and heat through. Serve on rolls with cabbage.

1 SANDWICH: 637 cal., 21g fat (6g sat. fat), 81mg chol., 864mg sod., 85g carb. (17g sugars, 5g fiber), 34g pro.

FREEZE OPTION

Freeze cooled pork mixture in freezer containers. To use, partially thaw in refrigerator overnight. Heat through in a covered saucepan, stirring occasionally; add broth if necessary.

For individual sandwiches at the ready, chill the cooked pork overnight. The following day, mound the pork in ½ - to 1-cup servings on a baking sheet. Cover and freeze. When frozen, pop the mounds off the sheet and store in a resealable freezer container. Then it's a cinch to reheat a serving in the microwave when you need a fast sandwich.

**BROWSE
10 NEW LAMB
CHOP RECIPES**
Just hover your
camera here.

BEST EVER LAMB CHOPS

My mom just loved a good lamb chop, and this easy recipe was her favorite way to have them. I've also grilled these chops with great results.
—Kim Mundy, Visalia, CA

PREP: 10 MIN. + CHILLING • **BROIL:** 10 MIN. • **MAKES:** 4 SERVINGS

1 tsp. each dried basil, marjoram and thyme
½ tsp. salt

8 lamb loin chops (3 oz. each)
Mint jelly, optional

1. Combine herbs and salt; rub over lamb chops. Cover and refrigerate for 1 hour.

2. Broil 4-6 in. from the heat until meat reaches desired doneness, 5-8 minutes on each side (for medium-rare, a thermometer should read 135°; medium, 140°; medium-well, 145°). Serve with mint jelly if desired.

2 LAMB CHOPS: 157 cal., 7g fat (2g sat. fat), 68mg chol., 355mg sod., 0 carb. (0 sugars, 0 fiber), 22g pro. **DIABETIC EXCHANGES:** 3 lean meat.

HONEY-GLAZED LAMB CHOPS

Omit step 1, herbs and salt. In a saucepan over medium-low heat, stir ⅓ cup each honey and prepared mustard and ⅛ tsp. each onion salt and pepper for 2-3 minutes or until honey is melted. Brush sauce over both sides of lamb. Proceed as directed in step 2.

LAMB
Tender and moist lamb lends itself to a variety of cooking methods and serving possibilities.

When Purchasing Lamb, Look For:
- A pinkish-red color.
- A package with no holes, tears or excessive liquid.
- A sell-by date later than the day of your purchase. If it is the same date, then use it that day or freeze it to cook later.

How Much To Purchase:
- 1 lb. bone-in roast = 2½ servings
- 1 lb. bone-in steaks = 2 servings
- 1 lb. bone-in ribs or loin chops = 2 servings
- 1 lb. rack of lamb = 2 servings

Defrosting Lamb:
The thicker the package, the longer it will take to thaw. Refer to these time guidelines when defrosting lamb in the refrigerator:

- For 1- to 1½-in.-thick packages of ground lamb or meat pieces, allow at least 24 hours.
- For 1-in.-thick chops, allow 12-14 hours.
- For a small roast, allow 3-5 hours per pound.
- For a large roast, allow 4-7 hours per pound.

SUNDAY POT ROAST

With the help of a slow cooker, you can prepare a down-home dinner any day of the week, not just on Sundays. The roast turns out tender and savory every time.
—Brandy Schaefer, Glen Carbon, IL

PREP: 10 MIN. + CHILLING • **COOK:** 8 HOURS • **MAKES:** 14 SERVINGS

1 tsp. dried oregano	6 medium carrots, peeled and cut into 1½-in. pieces
½ tsp. onion salt	3 large potatoes, peeled and quartered
½ tsp. caraway seeds	
½ tsp. pepper	3 small onions, quartered
¼ tsp. garlic salt	1½ cups beef broth
1 boneless pork loin roast (3½ to 4 lbs.), trimmed	⅓ cup all-purpose flour
	⅓ cup cold water
	¼ tsp. browning sauce, optional

1. Combine the first 5 ingredients; rub over the pork roast. Cover; refrigerate overnight.

2. Place carrots, potatoes and onions in a 6-qt. slow cooker; add broth. Place roast in slow cooker. Cook, covered, on low until meat and vegetables are tender, 8-10 hours.

3. Transfer roast and vegetables to a serving platter; tent with foil. Pour cooking juices into a small saucepan. Mix flour and water until smooth; stir into pan. Bring to a boil; cook and stir until thickened, about 2 minutes. If desired, add browning sauce. Serve roast with gravy and vegetables.

1 SERVING: 217 cal., 5g fat (2g sat. fat), 57mg chol., 230mg sod., 17g carb. (3g sugars, 2g fiber), 24g pro. **DIABETIC EXCHANGES:** 3 lean meat, 1½ starch.

HOW TO SPEED-PEEL CARROTS

Step 1: Hold carrot at a 45° angle on a cutting board. Start the vegetable peeler at the middle of the carrot and press downward toward the cutting board.

Step 2: Immediately switch directions and peel upward but only to the center of the carrot, rotating the carrot after you reach the starting point. Continue going up and down until bottom half of carrot is peeled.

Step 3: Flip carrot so the top is resting on the cutting board at a 45° angle and repeat.

PORK PURCHASING GUIDELINES

- Choose firm meat with a pink color and a small amount of surface fat.

- Package should have no holes, tears or excess liquid, which may indicate improper handling and storage.

- Ensure the sell-by date is later than the day of your purchase. If it is the same date, use the meat that day or freeze it for later.

- For the leanest pork options, opt for any cut from the loin.

**LEARN
ALL ABOUT
MAKING FRIED
RICE AT HOME**
Just hover your
camera here.

CHINESE PORK FRIED RICE

Here's an all-time classic scaled down for two. The peas and carrots add color and crunch to this savory dinner.
—Peggy Vaught, Glasgow, WV

TAKES: 25 MIN. • **MAKES:** 2 SERVINGS

1   boneless pork loin chop
    (6 oz.), cut into ½-in. pieces
¼   cup finely chopped carrot
¼   cup chopped fresh broccoli
¼   cup frozen peas
1   green onion, chopped
1   Tbsp. butter
1   large egg, lightly beaten
1   cup cold cooked long grain
    rice
4½ tsp. reduced-sodium soy
    sauce
⅛   tsp. garlic powder
⅛   tsp. ground ginger

1. In a large skillet, saute the pork, carrot, broccoli, peas and onion in butter until pork is no longer pink, 3-5 minutes. Remove from skillet and set aside.

2. In same skillet, cook and stir egg over medium heat until completely set. Stir in the rice, soy sauce, garlic powder, ginger and pork mixture; heat through. If desired, garnish with additional green onions.

1 CUP: 338 cal., 13g fat (6g sat. fat), 163mg chol., 597mg sod., 29g carb. (3g sugars, 2g fiber), 24g pro. **DIABETIC EXCHANGES:** 3 lean meat, 2 starch.

CHINESE PORK FRIED RICE TIPS

Can you make this Chinese pork fried rice recipe with other kinds of rice?
Fried rice is the perfect dish for using up leftover food. In fact, leftover rice is preferred in fried rice recipes because it has a lower moisture content than freshly cooked rice. You can use most types of rice in this Chinese pork fried rice recipe, but we typically use a long grain white.

What kind of skillet should you use to make this Chinese pork fried rice recipe? A wok is the traditional cookware for any dish requiring a stir-fry technique, but a nonstick skillet will also work well for making fried rice. A wide, flat skillet gives you more room to work with for cooking the eggs, incorporating other ingredients, and evenly cooking the rice.

What can you serve with Chinese pork fried rice? Fried rice pairs especially well with egg drop soup, a side of kimchi, egg rolls or some Sriracha sauce. Or cook up a batch of luscious Spicy BBQ Chicken Wings (p. 33).

USE A RICE COOKER TO MAKE PERFECT RICE EVERY TIME

Step 1: Rinse 1 cup rice under cool running water in a strainer. Wash rice until the water runs completely clear.

Step 2: Turn on rice cooker; add damp rice.

Step 3: Add water or broth according to the rice cooker's owner's manual. Rice cookers may require a bit less liquid than cooking on the stovetop, and different types of rice use slightly different ratios.

Step 4: Add ½ tsp. salt for each cup of dry rice.

Step 5: Stir everything with your paddle. Use your rice paddle to combine ingredients.

Note: Most rice cookers fully cook a batch of rice, whether 1 cup or more, in 30 to 40 minutes. If you're adding extra ingredients or alternative liquids, the time may differ slightly.

SIDES & CONDIMENTS

Let's celebrate the unsung heroes of mealtime: creamy mashed potatoes, crisp picnic salads and craveable refrigerator pickles. And don't forget crunchy homemade chips, holiday-worthy salads and sweet candied carrots.

BLUE CHEESE KALE SALAD

Instead of the standard spinach, romaine or iceberg, try kale in your salad! I didn't even like the leafy green until I made this recipe, and now I'm a total convert!
—Kathryn Egly, Colorado Springs, CO

TAKES: 20 MIN. • **MAKES:** 12 SERVINGS

- ½ cup olive oil
- 3 Tbsp. lime juice
- 2 Tbsp. honey
- ¼ tsp. salt
- ⅛ tsp. pepper
- 1 bunch kale (about 12 oz.), trimmed and chopped (about 14 cups)
- ½ cup sliced almonds, toasted
- ½ cup dried cranberries
- ½ cup shredded Parmesan cheese
- ½ cup crumbled blue cheese

In a small bowl, whisk the first 5 ingredients. Place kale in a large bowl. Drizzle with dressing; toss to coat. Top with remaining ingredients.

1¼ CUPS: 181 cal., 14g fat (3g sat. fat), 7mg chol., 183mg sod., 13g carb. (8g sugars, 1g fiber), 4g pro. **DIABETIC EXCHANGES:** 3 fat, 1 vegetable, ½ starch.

HOW TO MASSAGE TOUGH COOKING GREENS

To make tough kale or turnip greens more tender and palatable, place washed greens in a large bowl. Sprinkle with a little salt or olive oil if desired, then rub greens vigorously between your hands. After a few minutes, you'll have perfectly tender greens for your salad.

**ENJOY KALE
3 EASY WAYS**
Just hover your
camera here.

GINGERED CARROTS & PARSNIPS

Guests at my holiday table are surprised to hear that this tasty side dish has just five ingredients.
—Lucille Drake, Sherburne, NY

TAKES: 25 MIN. • **MAKES:** 6 SERVINGS

4 medium carrots, peeled and julienned
4 medium parsnips, peeled and julienned
2 Tbsp. chopped crystallized ginger, divided
2 Tbsp. butter
¼ tsp. salt

1. Place carrots and parsnips in a steamer basket; place in a large saucepan over 1 in. of water. Bring to a boil; cover and steam for 15-20 minutes or until crisp-tender.

2. In a large skillet, saute 1 Tbsp. ginger in butter for 1 minute. Add the carrots, parsnips and salt; toss to coat. Sprinkle with remaining ginger.

½ CUP: 153 cal., 4g fat (2g sat. fat), 10mg chol., 165mg sod., 29g carb. (10g sugars, 5g fiber), 2g pro. **DIABETIC EXCHANGES:** 2 starch, 1 fat.

DIG INTO PARSNIPS

Parsnips are a bit like herbaceous white carrots. Like carrots, parsnips are long, tapering root vegetables that grow deep underground. You'll find them in the fall or winter after the first frost.

Some farmers leave the parsips in the ground all winter and dig them up in spring. These parsnips are the sweetest, most candy-like root vegetables you'll ever taste, because the sugars have a chance to concentrate over the long overwintering process.

Look for small- to medium-sized parsnips, which are more sweet and tender than large, woody ones. If the parsnip is limp and soft, skip over it for a hearty, rigid root instead.

If you can't find parsnips, you can use all carrots in this recipe or substitute 2 medium turnips.

MOM'S POTATO PANCAKES

Old-fashioned potato pancakes are fluffy inside and crispy outside. Mom got this recipe from Grandma, so we've enjoyed it for years.
—Dianne Esposite, New Middletown, OH

TAKES: 30 MIN. • **MAKES:** 6 SERVINGS

4   cups shredded peeled
    potatoes (about 4 large
    potatoes)
1   large egg, lightly beaten
3   Tbsp. all-purpose flour
1   Tbsp. grated onion
1   tsp. salt
¼   tsp. pepper
    Oil for frying
    Optional: Chopped parsley,
    applesauce and sour cream

1. Rinse shredded potatoes in cold water; drain well, squeezing to remove excess water. Place in a large bowl. Stir in egg, flour, onion, salt and pepper.

2. In a large nonstick skillet, heat ¼ in. oil over medium heat. Working in batches, drop potato mixture by ⅓ cupfuls into oil; press to flatten slightly. Fry both sides until golden brown; drain on paper towels. Serve immediately. If desired, sprinkle with parsley and top with applesauce and sour cream.

2 PANCAKES: 171 cal., 7g fat (1g sat. fat), 31mg chol., 411mg sod., 24g carb. (1g sugars, 2g fiber), 3g pro.

**MASTER 6
WAYS TO COOK
POTATOES**
Just hover your
camera here.

REFRIGERATOR JALAPENO DILL PICKLES

I'm passionate about making pickles. My husband is passionate about eating them. He's too impatient to let them cure on the shelf, so I found this quick recipe to make him happy. Add hotter peppers if you'd like.
—Annie Jensen, Roseau, MN

PREP: 20 MIN. + CHILLING • **MAKES:** ABOUT 4 DOZEN PICKLE SPEARS

3 lbs. pickling cucumbers (about 12)
1 small onion, halved and sliced
¼ cup snipped fresh dill
1 to 2 jalapeno peppers, sliced
3 garlic cloves, minced
2½ cups water
2½ cups cider vinegar
⅓ cup canning salt
⅓ cup sugar

1. Cut each cucumber lengthwise into 4 spears. In a very large bowl, combine cucumbers, onion, dill, jalapenos and garlic. In a large saucepan, combine water, vinegar, salt and sugar. Bring to a boil; cook and stir just until salt and sugar are dissolved. Pour over cucumber mixture; cool.

2. Cover tightly and refrigerate for at least 24 hours. Store in the refrigerator for up to 2 months.

1 PICKLE SPEAR: 4 cal., 0 fat (0 sat. fat), 0 chol., 222mg sod., 1g carb. (0 sugars, 0 fiber), 0 pro.

HANDLING HOT PEPPERS

Wear disposable gloves when cutting hot peppers; the oils can burn skin. Avoid touching your face.

CAULIFLOWER MASH

When you want something fast, easy and definitely not ordinary for a weeknight dinner, try this mashed cauliflower side dish. It's a perfect (and tasty) substitute for mashed potatoes.
—*Taste of Home* Test Kitchen

TAKES: 20 MIN. • **MAKES:** 4 SERVINGS

1   medium head cauliflower, chopped (about 6 cups)
½   cup heavy whipping cream
¼   cup butter
1   tsp. whole peppercorns
2   garlic cloves, crushed
1   bay leaf
½   tsp. salt

1. In a large saucepan, cover cauliflower with water. Bring to a boil over medium-high heat. Reduce heat to low. Simmer, covered, until cauliflower is tender, 10-12 minutes; drain and return to pan.

2. Meanwhile, combine remaining ingredients in a small saucepan. Bring to a simmer over medium-low heat. Immediately remove from the heat and strain through a fine mesh strainer; discard the peppercorns, garlic and bay leaf.

3. Add cream mixture to cauliflower. Mash to reach desired consistency.

1 CUP: 243 cal., 23g fat (14g sat. fat), 64mg chol., 439mg sod., 9g carb. (4g sugars, 3g fiber), 4g pro.

SWEET CANDIED CARROTS

These tender, vibrant carrots have a buttery glaze and a mild sweetness. This is a simple dish, but it sure makes carrots seem special.
—P. Lauren Fay-Neri, Syracuse, NY

TAKES: 30 MIN. • **MAKES:** 8 SERVINGS

- 2 **lbs. carrots, sliced**
- ¼ **cup butter**
- ¼ **cup packed brown sugar**
- ¼ **tsp. salt**
- ⅛ **tsp. white pepper**
  Minced fresh parsley, optional

1. Place carrots in a large saucepan; add 1 in. water. Bring to a boil. Reduce heat; cover and simmer for 8-10 minutes or until crisp-tender. Drain and set aside.

2. In the same pan, combine the butter, brown sugar, salt and pepper; cook and stir until butter is melted. Return carrots to the pan; cook and stir over medium heat for 5 minutes or until glazed. If desired, sprinkle with parsley.

½ CUP: 125 cal., 6g fat (4g sat. fat), 15mg chol., 174mg sod., 18g carb. (14g sugars, 3g fiber), 1g pro.

SPICED CARROTS WITH PISTACHIOS VARIATION
Prepare the carrots as directed, stirring ½ cup golden raisins, ⅓ cup toasted pistachios and 1 tsp. apple pie spice into the brown sugar mixture.

CB'S CREAMY COLESLAW

This classic slaw is fantastic with spare ribs or pork roast and always hits the spot after a day of fishing on the Au Sable River in Michigan.
—Emily Tyra, Traverse City, MI

PREP: 15 MIN. + CHILLING • **MAKES:** 8 SERVINGS

1 **cup mayonnaise**	¼ **tsp. pepper**
⅓ **cup sugar**	¼ **tsp. paprika**
⅓ **cup white vinegar**	1 **lb. cabbage, cored and**
¼ **tsp. salt**	**chopped**

Whisk together first 6 ingredients until smooth. Toss cabbage with mayonnaise mixture. Refrigerate, covered, for 2 hours.

¾ CUP: 227 cal., 20g fat (3g sat. fat), 2mg chol., 224mg sod., 12g carb. (10g sugars, 1g fiber), 1g pro.

COLESLAW TIPS

- Purple cabbage can be used in this recipe, but it will make the dressing slightly purple as it sits.

- Coleslaws, whether creamy or vinegary, all taste better the longer they sit. Shoot for at least 2 hours of chilling, but 24 hours or longer for this chopped slaw is ideal.

- How you cut the cabbage helps determine how much water the cabbage will release when it sits. Chopped cabbage holds more water and stays crunchier over time.

- Don't forget to taste the slaw after it sits. It may need a little more salt and pepper.

- If you add onions to your slaw, go lightly. They intensify in flavor over time and can overpower the other ingredients.

A QUICK SHRED
You can shred the cabbage with a food processor or box grater. Finely shredded cabbage releases more water than chopped, so only chill it about an hour before serving.

GARLIC MASHED RED POTATOES TIPS

Can you use half-and-half instead of milk? If you've got a container of half-and-half in the fridge but are low on milk, you can use half-and-half in this recipe! You can also use heavy cream or full-fat milk for even richer mashed potatoes.

How do you fix having too much garlic in mashed potatoes? If you went a little heavy on the garlic, don't fret! You can add a little lemon juice to taste to counteract the strong garlic flavor. A small bit of sweetener, such as maple syrup or honey, can also help reverse a too-strong taste.

How do I make my mashed potatoes fluffy? For fluffy mashed potatoes, heat the milk and butter before adding them to the potatoes. Mash just until done.

GARLIC MASHED RED POTATOES

These creamy garlic mashed potatoes are so good, you can serve them plain—no butter or gravy is needed. This is the only way I make my mashed potatoes.
—Valerie Mitchell, Olathe, KS

TAKES: 30 MIN. • **MAKES:** 6 SERVINGS

8   medium red potatoes, quartered
3   garlic cloves, peeled
2   Tbsp. butter

½   cup fat-free milk, warmed
½   tsp. salt
¼   cup grated Parmesan cheese

1. Place potatoes and garlic in a large saucepan; cover with water. Bring to a boil. Reduce heat; cover and simmer for 15-20 minutes or until potatoes are very tender.

2. Drain well. Add the butter, milk and salt; mash. Stir in cheese.

1 CUP: 190 cal., 5g fat (3g sat. fat), 14mg chol., 275mg sod., 36g carb. (0 sugars, 4g fiber), 8g pro. **DIABETIC EXCHANGES:** 2 starch, ½ fat.

MAKE IT YOUR OWN

Now that you know the delicious basics, here are some insanely easy upgrades to mix up the tastiest mash:

• Add 2-3 Tbsp. of thinly sliced green onions, snipped chives or chopped parsley.

• Add 10-12 cloves of oven-roasted garlic, minced or smashed into a paste.

• Put the potatoes in an oven-safe dish, top with 2 Tbsp. of bread crumbs and 1 Tbsp. of grated Parmesan, and then broil until golden brown, 1-2 minutes.

WENDY'S APPLE POMEGRANATE SALAD

My grandparents grew pomegranates, pecans and walnuts and would send us some each year. Some of my best memories are the days I used to spend with my grandmother learning how to cook with them. Whenever I make this it's like having lunch with my grandmother again.
—Wendy G. Ball, Battle Creek, MI

TAKES: 20 MIN. • **MAKES:** 8 SERVINGS

1 bunch romaine, torn (about 8 cups)	1 large Granny Smith apple, chopped
½ cup pomegranate seeds	1 Tbsp. lemon juice
½ cup chopped pecans or walnuts, toasted	¼ cup olive oil
½ cup shredded Parmesan cheese	¼ cup white wine vinegar
	2 Tbsp. sugar
	¼ tsp. salt

1. In a large bowl, combine romaine, pomegranate seeds, pecans and cheese. Toss apple with lemon juice and add to salad.

2. In a small bowl, whisk remaining ingredients until blended. Drizzle over salad; toss to coat. Serve immediately.

1 CUP: 165 cal., 13g fat (2g sat. fat), 4mg chol., 163mg sod., 10g carb. (8g sugars, 2g fiber), 3g pro. **DIABETIC EXCHANGES:** 2½ fat, 1 vegetable.

GET TO KNOW POMEGRANATES

Flavor: Wondering what exotic-looking pomegranate tastes like? Pomegranate arils taste a lot like cranberries—fairly tart with a bit of sweetness underneath.

Storage: Refrigerate whole pomegranates in the fruit drawer for up to 2 weeks. The arils will keep in the refrigerator for about 3 days. You can also freeze them for 6 months.

Superfruit status: Pomegranates are some of the healthiest fruits on the planet, helping to lower blood pressure, risk of heart disease and cholesterol levels. They also offer anti-inflammatory benefits and may help fight some forms of cancer and arthritis.

HOW TO SEED A POMEGRANATE

Here's a simple way to get to those tart little gems inside a pomegranate. Enjoy them as a snack or as an addition to salads, roasts, drinks and more.

Cut the pomegranate in half. Hold it cut side down over a bowl of water, then, using a large spoon, give it a hearty smack on the skin. Keep smacking until all the seed pods—called arils—fall from the white membrane into the bowl. Discard the skin and membrane. Drain the water, reserving the arils. You can eat them whole, seeds and all.

BAKED POTATO CHIPS

These basic, crispy, baked chips are the perfect canvas for almost any meal. They are awesome for snacking.
—Mary Lou Kelly, Scottdale, PA

TAKES: 25 MIN. • **MAKES:** 2 SERVINGS

2 medium potatoes	½ tsp. salt
¼ cup olive oil	

1. Preheat oven to 425°. Cut potatoes into ⅛-in. slices; arrange in a single layer on 2 greased baking sheets. In a small bowl, mix oil and salt; brush over both sides of potatoes.

2. Roast until potatoes are tender, golden brown and crisp, 15-20 minutes, turning occasionally.

1 CUP: 403 cal., 27g fat (4g sat. fat), 0 chol., 603mg sod., 37g carb. (2g sugars, 4g fiber), 4g pro.

SERVE A LOADED POTATO DIP

In a large bowl, combine 2 cups sour cream, 1 cup finely shredded cheddar cheese, 1 envelope ranch salad dressing mix and 2-4 cooked and crumbled strips of bacon. Cover and refrigerate for at least 1 hour. Serve the dip with chips, crackers and/or vegetables.

PARMESAN-BREADED SQUASH

Yellow summer squash crisps beautifully when baked. You don't have to turn the pieces, but do keep an eye on them.
—Debi Mitchell, Flower Mound, TX

PREP: 20 MIN. • **BAKE:** 20 MIN. • **MAKES:** 6 SERVINGS

- 4 **cups thinly sliced yellow summer squash (3 medium)**
- 3 **Tbsp. olive oil**
- ½ **tsp. salt**
- ½ **tsp. pepper**
- ⅛ **tsp. cayenne pepper**
- ¾ **cup panko bread crumbs**
- ¾ **cup grated Parmesan cheese**

1. Preheat oven to 450°. Place squash in a large bowl. Add oil and seasonings; toss to coat.

2. In a shallow bowl, mix bread crumbs and cheese. Dip the squash in crumb mixture to coat both sides, patting to help coating adhere. Place on parchment-lined baking sheets. Bake 20-25 minutes or until golden brown, rotating pans halfway through baking.

⅔ CUP: 137 cal., 10g fat (2g sat. fat), 7mg chol., 346mg sod., 8g carb. (0 sugars, 2g fiber), 5g pro. **DIABETIC EXCHANGES:** 2 fat, 1 vegetable.

AIR-FRIED VARIATION

Preheat air fryer to 350°. Prepare squash.

In batches, arrange squash in a single layer on tray in air-fryer basket. Cook until squash is tender and coating is golden brown, about 10 minutes.

SUMMER SQUASH TIPS

Choosing: Look for summer squash that are firm and about 6 in. long and 2 in. in diameter. The skin should be glossy and prickly. Large squash can be tough and flavorless.

Storing: Keep unwashed squash in a perforated bag in the refrigerator for up to 5 days.

Prepping: Wash with cool water before preparing. The skin does not need to be peeled prior to eating.

SPRINGTIME POTATO SALAD

Traditional potato salad gets fun flavor from sweet pickles and a hearty crunch from celery and radishes in this recipe. I'm especially fond of the creamy dressing.
—Ellen Benninger, Greenville, PA

PREP: 20 MIN. + CHILLING • **MAKES:** 10 SERVINGS

6 cups cubed peeled potatoes
4 hard-boiled large eggs, chopped
1 celery rib, chopped
½ cup chopped sweet pickles
⅓ cup chopped onion
⅓ cup chopped radishes
½ cup mayonnaise
3 Tbsp. sugar
1 Tbsp. white vinegar
1 Tbsp. 2% milk
1½ tsp. prepared mustard
½ tsp. salt
Optional: Sliced green onions and paprika

1. Place potatoes in a saucepan and cover with water; bring to a boil. Reduce heat. Cook until tender, 10-15 minutes; drain. Place in a large bowl; add eggs, celery, pickles, onion and radishes.

2. In a small bowl, combine mayonnaise, sugar, vinegar, milk, mustard and salt; stir into potato mixture. Cover and refrigerate at least 1 hour before serving. If desired, garnish with green onions and paprika.

¾ CUP: 221 cal., 11g fat (2g sat. fat), 89mg chol., 297mg sod., 26g carb. (8g sugars, 2g fiber), 5g pro.

OLD BAY CRISPY KALE CHIPS

Here in East Hampton, New York, harvest time means big bunches of kale from local growers. These crunchy kale chips are delicious, super healthy and easy to make. I make them with seasoning to take the flavor up a notch. For extra zip, add a dash of cayenne pepper.
—Luanne Asta, Hampton Bays, NY

PREP: 10 MIN. • **BAKE:** 25 MIN. • **MAKES:** 4 SERVINGS

1 **bunch kale, washed**
2 **Tbsp. olive oil**
1 **to 3 tsp. Old Bay Seasoning**
   Sea salt, to taste

1. Preheat oven to 300°. Remove tough stems from kale and tear leaves into large pieces. Place in a large bowl. Toss with olive oil and seasonings. Arrange leaves in a single layer on greased baking sheets.

2. Bake, uncovered, 10 minutes and then rotate pans. Continue baking until crisp and just starting to brown, about 15 minutes longer. Let stand at least 5 minutes before serving.

1 SERVING: 101 cal., 7g fat (1g sat. fat), 0 chol., 202mg sod., 8g carb. (0 sugars, 2g fiber), 3g pro. **DIABETIC EXCHANGES:** 1½ fat, 1 vegetable.

LEARN THE
STEPS TO
CHARCUTERIE
BOARD
PERFECTION
Just hover your
camera here.

PICKLED CAULIFLOWER

My mother makes the finest bread and butter pickles I've ever had. I wanted to create a different recipe using her brine on the copious heads of cauliflower that we harvest each year. This pickled cauliflower is particularly wonderful in the fall served with roasts and chops, or tossed into a salad with spinach, apples and nuts.
—Jennifer Beckman, Falls Church, VA

PREP TIME: 25 MIN. + CHILLING • **MAKES:** 32 SERVINGS

- 2 small heads cauliflower, cut into florets
- ½ large sweet onion, halved and sliced
- 2 cups white vinegar
- 1 cup water
- 1 cup sugar
- ¼ cup canning salt
- 1 tsp. mustard seed
- 1 tsp. crushed red pepper flakes
- ½ tsp. celery seed
- ½ tsp. ground turmeric

Place cauliflower and onion in a large bowl. In a saucepan, combine the remaining ingredients. Bring to a boil; reduce heat and simmer until sugar dissolves, 1-2 minutes. Pour over cauliflower; cool. Transfer to jars, if desired; seal tightly. Refrigerate at least 2 hours before serving. Store in the refrigerator for up to 2 months.

¼ CUP: 11 cal., 0 fat (0 sat. fat), 0 chol., 47mg sod., 2g carb. (2g sugars, 0 fiber), 0 pro.

MAKE IT YOUR OWN

Serve these surprising pickles on a charcuterie board with salami or summer sausage, prosciutto or country ham, sliced Swiss or Gouda cheese, a mild blue cheese and pimiento-stuffed olives.

FIESTA CHOPPED SALAD

We serve this colorful garden feast when we find vegetables that are bursting with flavor.
The dressing makes the fresh salad a welcome addition to most any entree.
—Merwyn Garbini, Tucson, AZ

TAKES: 30 MIN. • **MAKES:** 8 SERVINGS

- 1 **medium sweet red pepper, chopped**
- 1 **medium sweet yellow pepper, chopped**
- 1 **medium tomato, seeded and chopped**
- 1 **medium cucumber, seeded and chopped**
- 1 **small zucchini, chopped**
- 2 **green onions, chopped**
- 2 **Tbsp. minced fresh parsley**
- 2 **Tbsp. olive oil**
- 1 **Tbsp. red wine vinegar**
- ½ **tsp. sugar**
- ¼ **tsp. salt**
- ¼ **tsp. pepper**
- 1 **large ripe avocado, peeled and chopped**
- 1 **Tbsp. lemon juice**

In a large bowl, combine the first 7 ingredients. In a small bowl, whisk the oil, vinegar, sugar, salt and pepper. Drizzle over vegetables and toss to coat. Toss avocado with lemon juice; gently fold into salad. Serve with a slotted spoon.

½ CUP: 91 cal., 7g fat (1g sat. fat), 0 chol., 81mg sod., 7g carb. (0 sugars, 2g fiber), 1g pro. **DIABETIC EXCHANGES:** 1½ fat, 1 vegetable.

CHOP, CHOP

Chopped salads are easy to serve and eat because the foods are chopped into (or presented in) uniform-size shapes. So, making a chopped salad is a great way to hone your knife skills (learn more on p. 4).

To make chopped salads more hearty, add drained and rinsed canned beans or cubed cooked ham to them.

BREAKFAST & BRUNCH

The most important meal of the day is also packed with chances to shine in the kitchen. Whip up classic omelets, Benedicts and waffles, plus trendy smoothie bowls, cold-brew coffee and meal preps. Good mornings start here!

ULTIMATE FRENCH TOAST

There's no question that this is the best French toast recipe. The caramelized exterior meets a soft, custardlike center that practically melts in your mouth. Not only that, but it's quick and easy too!
—Audrey Rompon, Milwaukee, WI

TAKES: 15 MIN. • **MAKES:** 4 SERVINGS

1½ cups half-and-half cream	8 slices day-old brioche bread (1 in. thick)
3 large egg yolks	Optional toppings: Butter, maple syrup, fresh berries, whipped cream and confectioners' sugar
3 Tbsp. brown sugar	
2 tsp. vanilla extract	
¾ tsp. ground cinnamon	
½ tsp. salt	
¼ tsp. ground nutmeg	

1. In a shallow dish, whisk together the first 7 ingredients. Preheat a greased griddle over medium heat.

2. Dip bread into egg mixture, letting it soak 5 seconds on each side. Cook on griddle until golden brown on both sides. Serve with toppings as desired.

2 PIECES: 546 cal., 24g fat (15g sat. fat), 263mg chol., 786mg sod., 64g carb. (25g sugars, 2g fiber), 13g pro.

TEST KITCHEN TIP

Using day-old bread from a bakery helps the French toast to keep its shape. If you're using commercially produced brioche, be sure to allow the bread to become slightly stale for best results.

AIR-FRIED VARIATION
Preheat air fryer to 400°. Prepare quiche cups; place ramekins on tray in air-fryer basket. Cook until a knife inserted in the center comes out clean, 20-25 minutes.

BACON-BROCCOLI QUICHE CUPS

Chock-full of veggies and melted cheese, this comforting and colorful egg bake has become a holiday brunch classic at our house. For a tasty variation, substitute asparagus for broccoli and Swiss for cheddar cheese.
—Irene Steinmeyer, Denver, CO

PREP: 10 MIN. • **BAKE:** 25 MIN. • **MAKES:** 2 SERVINGS

4 **bacon strips, chopped**
¼ **cup small fresh broccoli florets**
¼ **cup chopped onion**
1 **garlic clove, minced**
3 **large eggs**
1 **Tbsp. dried parsley flakes**
⅛ **tsp. seasoned salt**
   Dash pepper
¼ **cup shredded cheddar cheese**
2 **Tbsp. chopped tomato**

1. Preheat oven to 400°. In a skillet, cook bacon over medium heat until crisp, stirring occasionally. Remove bacon with a slotted spoon; drain on paper towels. Pour off drippings, reserving 2 tsp. in pan.

2. Add broccoli and onion to drippings in pan; cook and stir 2-3 minutes or until tender. Add garlic; cook 1 minute longer.

3. In a small bowl, whisk eggs, parsley, seasoned salt and pepper until blended. Stir in cheese, tomato, bacon and the broccoli mixture.

4. Divide the mixture evenly between 2 greased 10-oz. ramekins or custard cups. Bake until a knife inserted in the center comes out clean, 22-25 minutes.

1 SERVING: 302 cal., 23g fat (9g sat. fat), 314mg chol., 597mg sod., 5g carb. (2g sugars, 1g fiber), 19g pro.

FREEZE OPTION

Cover and freeze unbaked quiche cups. To use, remove from freezer 30 minutes before baking (do not thaw). Bake as directed, increasing time as necessary for a knife inserted in the center to come out clean. Cover loosely with foil if tops brown too quickly.

CRUNCHY GRANOLA

This crisp, lightly sweet mixture is great just eaten out of hand or as an ice cream topping. My husband and I grow wheat, barley and canola.
—Lorna Jacobsen, Arrowwood, AB

PREP: 15 MIN. • **BAKE:** 30 MIN. + COOLING • **MAKES:** 8 CUPS

⅔ cup honey
½ cup canola oil
⅓ cup packed brown sugar
2 tsp. vanilla extract
4 cups old-fashioned oats
1 cup sliced almonds

1 cup sweetened shredded coconut
½ cup sesame seeds
½ cup salted sunflower kernels
2 cups raisins

1. Preheat oven to 300°. In a small saucepan, combine honey, oil and brown sugar; cook and stir over medium heat until sugar is dissolved. Remove from the heat; stir in vanilla.

2. In a large bowl, combine oats, almonds, coconut, sesame seeds and sunflower kernels. Add honey mixture, stirring until evenly coated. Spread onto 2 greased 15x10x1-in. baking pans.

3. Bake 20 minutes, stirring frequently. Stir in raisins. Bake until lightly toasted, about 10 minutes longer. Cool completely in pans on wire racks, stirring occasionally. Store in an airtight container.

½ **CUP:** 366 cal., 18g fat (3g sat. fat), 0 chol., 51mg sod., 50g carb. (30g sugars, 5g fiber), 6g pro.

CRUNCHY GRANOLA TIPS

What else can you add to this crunchy granola recipe? Stir semisweet or dark chocolate morsels into the cooled granola. You can also stir any dried fruit, such as dried cherries or chopped dried apricots, into this recipe. Replace the almonds with your favorite kind of nut.

How can you get perfect granola clusters? To make clusters, stir homemade granola only occasionally when it's baking. Use a gentle folding motion to keep granola in larger chunks. You can also compress the warm mixture, still on the baking pan, with your hands to help form clusters.

How can you make this granola recipe healthier? Use unsweetened coconut flakes instead of sweetened to pare back a bit on sugar. You could also increase the oats to 5 cups and almonds to 1¼ cups, which will make more granola with less added sugar per serving. Use a variety of dried fruits—dried goji berries, blueberries and cranberries add a shot of color and antioxidants.

**LEARN MORE
ABOUT THE
MEDITERRANEAN
DIET**
Just hover your
camera here.

MEDITERRANEAN OMELET

This fluffy omelet gives us reason to rush to the breakfast table. For extra flair,
add some chopped fresh herbs like basil, oregano or tarragon.
—Milynne Charlton, Scarborough, ON

TAKES: 10 MIN. • **MAKES:** 2 SERVINGS

4 **large eggs**
¼ **cup water**
⅛ **tsp. salt**
   Dash pepper
1 **Tbsp. butter**
¼ **cup crumbled feta or**
   goat cheese
¼ **cup chopped tomato**
1 **green onion, chopped**

1. In a small bowl, whisk eggs, water, salt and pepper until blended. In a large nonstick skillet, heat butter over medium-high heat. Pour in egg mixture. Mixture should set immediately at edge. As eggs set, push cooked portions toward the center, letting uncooked eggs flow underneath.

2. When eggs are thickened and no liquid egg remains, add cheese, tomato and green onion to 1 side. Fold omelet in half; slide onto a plate. Cut into 2 portions.

½ OMELET: 236 cal., 18g fat (8g sat. fat), 395mg chol., 472mg sod., 3g carb. (1g sugars, 1g fiber), 15g pro.

CLASSIC AVOCADO TOAST

This is such an easy way to add avocados to your diet. Use healthy multigrain bread and add toppings like sliced radishes and cracked pepper or minced chipotle peppers and fresh cilantro leaves.
—*Taste of Home* Test Kitchen

TAKES: 5 MIN. • **MAKES:** 1 SERVING

1 slice hearty bread, toasted
1 to 2 tsp. extra virgin olive oil
 or coconut oil
¼ medium ripe avocado, sliced
⅛ tsp. sea salt
 Optional: Sliced radishes
 and cracked black pepper

Spread toast with olive oil; top with avocado slices. If desired, mash avocado slightly and drizzle with additional oil. Sprinkle with salt. Top with radishes and cracked pepper if desired.

1 SLICE: 160 cal., 11g fat (2g sat. fat), 0 chol., 361mg sod., 15g carb. (1g sugars, 3g fiber), 3g pro. **DIABETIC EXCHANGES:** 2 fat, 1 starch.

AVOCADOS FOR THE WIN

Packed with vitamins C and B6, magnesium and potassium, avocados are nutrition superstars.

Purchasing: Ripe avocados give slightly to gentle pressure, and their stems come off easily. Hass avocados will turn dark green or black, while other varieties may stay light green.

Ripening at home: Place in a bag with a banana or apple. (See p. 16.)

Storing: Keep ripe avocados at room temperature. Once cut into, sprinkle them with fresh lime juice or vinegar and refrigerate, tightly covered, for up to 3 days.

Freezing: Pop sliced or cubed avocado into a freezer container to use later in smoothies, sauces or guacamole.

SMOKED SALMON EGG SALAD

Smoked salmon and croissants elevate egg salad sandwiches to a delicious and decidedly grown-up level.
—Cathy Tang, Redmond, WA

TAKES: 10 MIN. • **MAKES:** 6 SERVINGS

¾ cup mayonnaise	6 hard-boiled large eggs, chopped
1 tsp. dill weed	4 oz. smoked salmon, chopped
½ tsp. lemon juice	6 croissants, split
¼ tsp. salt	1½ cups fresh baby spinach
⅛ tsp. pepper	

1. In a large bowl, combine the first 5 ingredients. Stir in the eggs and salmon.

2. Place ⅓ cup on the bottom of each croissant; top with spinach leaves and replace croissant tops.

1 SANDWICH: 533 cal., 40g fat (11g sat. fat), 265mg chol., 889mg sod., 27g carb. (7g sugars, 2g fiber), 15g pro.

HARD-BOILED EGGS TIPS

How do you know when boiled eggs are done? Use a timer. For firm yolks, boil the eggs for 12 minutes; for hard yolks, go for 15 minutes.

Why are my hard-boiled eggs hard to peel? The most likely reason is that the eggs are too fresh. The shells of fresh eggs will chip much more than eggs that have been in your fridge for several days. So always use older eggs for easier peeling.

How long can you keep hard-boiled eggs in the refrigerator? Hard-boiled eggs with the shell on last about a week in the fridge when stored in an airtight container. Once peeled, the eggs should be enjoyed the same day.

IMPROVISED EGG CHOPPER

Use a grid-style cooling rack to "chop" hard-boiled eggs. It's faster (and less slippery) than using a knife. Set the rack on top of a bowl and smoosh the peeled egg through.

POWER BERRY SMOOTHIE BOWL

While you can't taste the spinach in these smoothies, you get all its nutrients with big berry flavor.
—Christine Hair, Odessa, FL

TAKES: 10 MIN. • **MAKES:** 3 SERVINGS

½ cup orange juice
½ cup pomegranate juice
1 container (6 oz.) mixed berry yogurt
1 cup frozen unsweetened strawberries
1 cup fresh baby spinach
½ medium ripe frozen banana, sliced
½ cup frozen unsweetened blueberries
2 Tbsp. ground flaxseed
Optional: Sliced fresh strawberries, fresh blueberries, flaxseed and granola

In a blender, combine the first 8 ingredients; cover and process for 30 seconds or until smooth. Pour into chilled bowls; top as desired. Serve immediately.

1 CUP: 172 cal., 3g fat (0 sat. fat), 3mg chol., 47mg sod., 35g carb. (28g sugars, 4g fiber), 5g pro.

POWER UP WITH HEALTHY SMOOTHIES

Sneak our favorite power foods into your new go-to breakfast.

- **Berries:** for bright flavor, fiber and healthy antioxidants. Include some frozen cranberries for extra zing!

- **Avocado:** makes it so rich and creamy

- **Protein powder:** a nutrition boost that helps you feel full

- **Spinach:** the simplest way to make veggies disappear

- **Flaxseed:** for omega-3s, protein and fiber

- **Kefir:** packed with even more belly-friendly bugs than yogurt

POTATO SAUSAGE FRITTATA

With sausage, bacon, eggs and potatoes, this frittata is one hearty meal! Although I double the recipe for my large family, we never have any leftovers. As good as this dish is, you can experiment to customize it for your family. Try using ham, bell peppers, chorizo—the sky's the limit!
—Patricia Lee, Eatonton, GA

TAKES: 30 MIN. • **MAKES:** 4 SERVINGS

½ **lb. bulk pork sausage**
6 **bacon strips, diced**
1½ **cups finely chopped red potatoes**
1 **medium onion, finely chopped**

8 **large eggs**
2 **tsp. dried parsley flakes**
¾ **tsp. salt**
⅛ **tsp. pepper**

1. In a large cast-iron or other ovenproof skillet, cook sausage over medium heat until no longer pink. Remove and set aside. In the same skillet, cook bacon over medium heat until crisp. Using a slotted spoon, remove to paper towels; drain, reserving 2 Tbsp. drippings.

2. In the drippings, saute potatoes and onion until tender. In a large bowl, whisk the eggs, parsley, salt and pepper. Return sausage and bacon to the skillet; top with egg mixture.

3. Cover and cook over low heat until eggs are almost set, 8-10 minutes. Uncover; broil 6 in. from the heat until eggs are set, about 2 minutes. Cut into wedges.

1 PIECE: 518 cal., 39g fat (13g sat. fat), 430mg chol., 1213mg sod., 16g carb. (3g sugars, 2g fiber), 25g pro.

CORN CAKES WITH POACHED EGGS & MANGO SALSA

Don't be intimidated by the poached eggs in this bright, can't-miss morning meal.
—Eva Amuso, Cheshire, MA

PREP: 40 MIN. • **COOK:** 5 MIN./BATCH • **MAKES:** 6 SERVINGS

1 medium mango, peeled and chopped
½ cup salsa
2 Tbsp. minced fresh cilantro
1 green onion, finely chopped

CORN CAKES
4 large eggs, room temperature
⅔ cup all-purpose flour
⅔ cup cornmeal
4 tsp. baking powder
1 tsp. salt
⅛ tsp. pepper
1 can (8¼ oz.) cream-style corn
½ cup 2% milk
½ cup butter, melted
1 cup fresh or frozen corn, thawed
4 green onions, chopped
¼ tsp. cream of tartar

POACHED EGGS
1 Tbsp. white vinegar
6 large eggs

1. In a small bowl, combine the mango, salsa, cilantro and onion; set aside.

2. Separate 2 eggs. In a large bowl, combine the flour, cornmeal, baking powder, salt and pepper. In another bowl, whisk the remaining eggs, egg yolks, cream-style corn, milk and butter. Stir into dry ingredients just until blended. Fold in corn and onions. In a small bowl, beat egg whites and cream of tartar until stiff peaks form. Fold into batter.

3. Pour batter by ¼ cupfuls onto a greased cast-iron skillet or hot griddle. Cook until golden brown, 2-3 minutes on each side.

4. Meanwhile, place 2-3 in. water in a large skillet with high sides; add vinegar. Bring to a boil; reduce heat and simmer gently. Break cold eggs, 1 at a time, into a custard cup or saucer; holding the cup close to the surface of the water, slip each egg into water.

5. Cook, uncovered, until whites are completely set and yolks are still soft, about 4 minutes. With a slotted spoon, lift eggs out of water. Serve with corn cakes and salsa.

1 SERVING: 455 cal., 25g fat (13g sat. fat), 392mg chol., 1097mg sod., 45g carb. (10g sugars, 4g fiber), 16g pro.

HOW TO POACH EGGS

Here's how to make perfectly poached eggs every time.

Step 1: Place 2-3 in. water in a deep skillet or saucepan; bring it to a boil. Add 1 Tbsp. white vinegar and ¾ tsp. salt. Lower heat so water no longer boils but bubbles are gently springing from bottom of pan.

Step 2: Break cold eggs, 1 at a time, into ramekins or small bowls. Don't crack the eggs directly into the water—the less disturbed the egg is as you drop it in, the better.

Step 3: Gently stir the water in a clockwise motion. Hold egg bowl over water as close as you comfortably can; gently slip egg into water. Give it a few seconds to gather together before adding a second egg (for best results, don't cook more than 2 at a time).

Step 4: Cook, uncovered, until the whites are set and opaque and the yolks begin to thicken but are not hard, 3-5 minutes. Lift eggs out of water with a slotted spoon.

STRAWBERRY CREPES TIPS

Can you fold and stack crepes instead of rolling them up? If you're having a hard time rolling up the crepes, you can fold them instead. Fill and fold in half, then fold again 1 or 2 more times to create a wedge-shaped crepe. You can stack these crepes on top of each other without smearing the filling (great for working ahead and storing in the fridge!) Also, be careful not to overcook the crepes—that will make them less pliable.

Can you use frozen strawberries instead? No. We recommend using fresh strawberries—or a blend of fresh berries like raspberries, blueberries and blackberries—for this recipe. Thawed frozen berries will bleed into the white filling.

How can you make these crepes your own? There are so many tasty ways to level up your strawberry crepes! Drizzle them with some chocolate sauce, add Nutella to the filling, top with confectioners' sugar or serve with a dollop of homemade whipped cream.

STRAWBERRY CREPES

Wrap summer-ripe strawberries and creamy filling into these delicate crepes for an elegant brunch entree.
—Kathy Kochiss, Huntington, CT

PREP: 15 MIN. + CHILLING • **COOK:** 25 MIN. • **MAKES:** 7 SERVINGS

4 **large eggs**	1¼ **cups confectioners' sugar**
1 **cup 2% milk**	1 **Tbsp. lemon juice**
1 **cup water**	1 **tsp. grated lemon zest**
2 **Tbsp. butter, melted**	½ **tsp. vanilla extract**
2 **cups all-purpose flour**	4 **cups fresh strawberries, sliced, divided**
¼ **tsp. salt**	1 **cup heavy whipping cream, whipped**

FILLING
1 **pkg. (8 oz.) cream cheese, softened**

1. In a large bowl, whisk eggs, milk, water and butter. In another bowl, mix flour and salt; add to egg mixture and mix well. Refrigerate, covered, 1 hour.

2. Heat a lightly greased 8-in. nonstick skillet over medium heat. Stir batter. Fill a ¼-cup measure halfway with batter; pour into center of pan. Quickly lift and tilt pan to coat bottom evenly. Cook until top appears dry; turn crepe over and cook until bottom is cooked, 15-20 seconds longer. Remove to a wire rack. Repeat with remaining batter, greasing pan as needed. When cool, stack crepes between pieces of waxed paper or paper towels.

3. For filling, in a small bowl, beat cream cheese, confectioners' sugar, lemon juice and zest, and vanilla until smooth. Fold in 2 cups berries and the whipped cream. Spoon about ⅓ cup filling down the center of each crepe; roll up. Garnish with remaining berries and, if desired, additional confectioners' sugar. Cover and refrigerate or freeze remaining crepes in an airtight container, unfilled, for another use.

2 CREPES: 415 cal., 26g fat (16g sat. fat), 115mg chol., 163mg sod., 40g carb. (28g sugars, 2g fiber), 7g pro.

HOMEMADE YOGURT

You'll be surprised how easy it is to make homemade yogurt. Top it with granola and your favorite berries.
—*Taste of Home* Test Kitchen

PREP: 5 MIN. • **COOK:** 20 MIN. + STANDING • **MAKES:** ABOUT 2 QT.

2 qt. pasteurized whole milk	2 Tbsp. plain yogurt with live active cultures

1. In a Dutch oven, heat milk over medium heat until a thermometer reads 200°, stirring occasionally to prevent scorching. Remove from heat; let stand until a thermometer reads 112°-115°, stirring occasionally. (If desired, place pan in an ice-water bath for faster cooling.)

2. Whisk 1 cup warm milk into yogurt until smooth; return all to pan, stirring gently. Transfer mixture to warm, clean jars, such as 1-qt. canning jars.

3. Cover jars; place in oven. Turn on oven light to keep mixture warm, about 110°. Let stand, undisturbed, until yogurt is set, 6-24 hours, tilting jars gently to check consistency. (Yogurt will become thicker and more tangy as it stands.)

4. Refrigerate, covered, until cold. Store in refrigerator up to 2 weeks.

1 CUP: 151 cal., 8g fat (5g sat. fat), 25mg chol., 107mg sod., 12g carb. (12g sugars, 0 fiber), 8g pro. **DIABETIC EXCHANGES:** 1 whole milk.

YOGURT-MAKING TIPS

Make sure the oven maintains a steady temperature around 110°. Small lumps can form if the temperature gets too high. You can also incubate yogurt inside a slow cooker set to low or wrapped in a heating pad. Check periodically to ensure the temperature is right and consistent.

Gently tilt the jars to test whether yogurt has set. (It will thicken further when you refrigerate it.) When the consistency is to your liking, whisk yogurt to form a smooth, creamy texture. Cover the finished yogurt and pop it into the fridge until cold. It'll keep for up to 2 weeks.

Be sure to save 2 Tbsp. of your homemade yogurt—you can use it as a starter for your next batch! This starter will freeze well, too, if you can't make more yogurt right away.

DENVER OMELET SALAD

I love this recipe. It's not your typical breakfast, but it has all the right elements. Plus, it's healthy and fast. Turn your favorite omelet ingredients into a morning salad!
—Pauline Custer, Duluth, MN

TAKES: 25 MIN. • **MAKES:** 4 SERVINGS

8 **cups fresh baby spinach**
1 **cup chopped tomatoes**
2 **Tbsp. olive oil, divided**
1½ **cups chopped fully cooked ham**
1 **small onion, chopped**
1 **small green pepper, chopped**
4 **large eggs**
  Salt and pepper to taste

1. Arrange spinach and tomatoes on a platter; set aside. In a large skillet, heat 1 Tbsp. olive oil over medium-high heat. Add ham, onion and green pepper; saute until ham is heated through and vegetables are tender, 5-7 minutes. Spoon over spinach and tomatoes.

2. In same skillet, heat remaining olive oil over medium heat. Break eggs, 1 at a time, into a small cup, then gently slide into skillet. Immediately reduce heat to low; season with salt and pepper. To prepare sunny-side up eggs, cover pan and cook until whites are completely set and yolks thicken but are not hard. Top salad with fried eggs.

1 SERVING: 229 cal., 14g fat (3g sat. fat), 217mg chol., 756mg sod., 7g carb. (3g sugars, 2g fiber), 20g pro. **DIABETIC EXCHANGES:** 3 lean meat, 2 fat, 1 vegetable.

MAKE IT YOUR OWN

Consider these restaurant-inspired omelet salads:

- **Everything Omelet Salad:** Add sliced mushrooms to the ham and veggie mixture; sprinkle salad with shredded cheddar cheese.

- **Mushroom & Swiss Omelet Salad:** Substitute sliced baby portobello mushrooms for the ham; omit green pepper (and onion, if desired). Sprinkle salad with shredded Swiss cheese.

- **Omelet Lorraine Salad:** Omit ham and green pepper. Cook and crumble 6 bacon strips; caramelize 1 medium onion, chopped, in 1 Tbsp. drippings. Sprinkle bacon and onion over spinach mixture; top with eggs and shredded Swiss cheese.

COLD-BREW COFFEE

Cold-brewing reduces the acidity of coffee, which enhances its natural sweetness and complex flavors. Even those who take hot coffee with sugar and cream might find themselves sipping cold brew plain.
—*Taste of Home* Test Kitchen

PREP: 10 MIN. + CHILLING • **MAKES:** 8 SERVINGS

1 cup coarsely ground medium-roast coffee
1 cup hot water (205°)
6 to 7 cups cold water
Optional: 2% milk or half-and-half cream

1. Place the coffee grounds in a clean glass container. Pour hot water over the grounds; let stand 10 minutes. Stir in cold water. Cover and refrigerate 12-24 hours. (The longer the coffee sits, the stronger the flavor.)

2. Strain coffee through a fine-mesh sieve; discard grounds. Strain coffee again through a coffee filter; discard grounds. Serve over ice, with milk or cream if desired. Store in the refrigerator for up to 2 weeks.

1 CUP: 2 cal., 0 fat (0 sat. fat), 0 chol., 4mg sod., 0 carb. (0 sugars, 0 fiber), 0 pro.

COLD-BREW COFFEE TIPS

• While many cold-brew recipes don't use any hot water, we like the effect it has on the coffee. The near-boiling water releases carbon dioxide in the grounds, extracting more flavor from the beans.

• Some people enjoy a tiny pinch of salt instead of sugar in cold brews. Salt brings out the coffee's inherent sweetness.

• Freeze some coffee in ice cube trays. The frozen coffee cubes will chill your beverage without watering it down.

FREEZE & STORE

Wrap the individual sandwiches in waxed paper, and then in foil before freezing. The foil protects them from freezer burn; the waxed paper allows for mess-free reheating and eating on the go.

FREEZER BREAKFAST SANDWICHES

On a busy morning, these freezer breakfast sandwiches save the day. A hearty combo of eggs, Canadian bacon and cheese will keep you fueled through lunchtime and beyond.
—Christine Rukavena, Milwaukee, WI

PREP: 25 MIN. • **BAKE:** 15 MIN. • **MAKES:** 12 SANDWICHES

12 **large eggs**
⅔ **cup 2% milk**
½ **tsp. salt**
¼ **tsp. pepper**

SANDWICHES
12 **English muffins, split**
4 **Tbsp. butter, softened**
12 **slices Colby-Monterey Jack cheese**
12 **slices Canadian bacon**

1. Preheat oven to 325°. In a large bowl, whisk eggs, milk, salt and pepper until blended. Pour into a 13x9-in. baking pan coated with cooking spray. Bake until set, 15-18 minutes. Cool on a wire rack.

2. Meanwhile, toast English muffins (or bake at 325° until lightly browned, 12-15 minutes). Spread 1 tsp. butter on each muffin bottom.

3. Cut eggs into 12 portions. Layer muffin bottoms with an egg portion, a cheese slice (tearing cheese to fit) and Canadian bacon. Replace muffin tops. Wrap sandwiches in waxed paper and then in foil; freeze in a freezer container.

4. To use frozen sandwiches: Remove foil. Microwave a waxed paper-wrapped sandwich at 50% power until thawed, 1-2 minutes. Turn sandwich over; microwave at 100% power until hot and a thermometer reads at least 160°, 30-60 seconds. Let stand 2 minutes before serving.

1 SANDWICH: 334 cal., 17g fat (9g sat. fat), 219mg chol., 759mg sod., 26g carb. (3g sugars, 2g fiber), 19g pro.

SPARKLING PEACH BELLINIS

Folks will savor the subtle peach flavor in this elegant brunch beverage.
—Taste of Home Test Kitchen

PREP: 35 MIN. + COOLING • **MAKES:** 12 SERVINGS

3 **medium peaches, halved**	2 **bottles (750 ml each)**
1 **Tbsp. honey**	**champagne or sparkling**
1 **can (11.3 oz.) peach nectar,**	**grape juice, chilled**
chilled	

1. Preheat oven to 375°. Line a baking sheet with a large piece of heavy-duty foil (about 18x12 in.). Place peach halves, cut sides up, on foil; drizzle with honey. Fold foil over peaches and seal.

2. Bake for 25-30 minutes or until tender. Cool completely; remove and discard peels. In a food processor, process peaches until smooth.

3. Transfer peach puree to a pitcher. Add the nectar and 1 bottle of champagne; stir until combined. Pour into 12 champagne flutes or wine glasses; top with remaining champagne. Serve immediately.

¾ CUP: 74 cal., 0 fat (0 sat. fat), 0 chol., 2mg sod., 9g carb. (7g sugars, 1g fiber), 0 pro.

GET CREATIVE

1) Beermosa: Pour 2 oz. orange juice into a champagne flute or wine glass; top with 3 oz. Belgian-style white beer.

2) Blue Lagoon Mimosa: Pour 2 oz. lemonade and ½ oz. blue curacao into a champagne flute or wine glass; top with 3 oz. champagne.

3) Pomegranate Mimosa: Pour 1 oz. pomegranate juice and 1 oz. pomegranate liqueur into a champagne flute or wine glass; top with 3 oz. champagne.

HOW TO TEST DONENESS OF HOLLANDAISE

Dip a spoon in the sauce and run your finger across the back. A fully cooked sauce will hold a firm line and not run down.

EGGS BENEDICT WITH HOMEMADE HOLLANDAISE

Legend has it that poached eggs on an English muffin started at Delmonico's in New York. Here's my take on this brunch classic, and don't spare the hollandaise.
—Barbara Pletzke, Herndon, VA

TAKES: 30 MIN. • **MAKES:** 8 SERVINGS

4 large egg yolks
2 Tbsp. water
2 Tbsp. lemon juice
¾ cup butter, melted
    Dash white pepper

ASSEMBLY
8 large eggs
4 English muffins, split and toasted
8 slices Canadian bacon, warmed
    Paprika

1. For hollandaise sauce, in top of a double boiler or in a metal bowl over simmering water, whisk egg yolks, water and lemon juice until blended; cook until the mixture is just thick enough to coat a metal spoon and temperature reaches 160°, whisking constantly. Remove from heat. Very slowly drizzle in warm melted butter, whisking constantly. Whisk in white pepper. Transfer to a small bowl if necessary. Place bowl in a larger bowl of warm water. Keep warm, stirring occasionally, until ready to serve, up to 30 minutes.

2. Place 2-3 in. water in a large saucepan or skillet with high sides. Bring to a boil; adjust heat to maintain a gentle simmer. Break 1 egg into a small bowl; holding bowl close to surface of water, slip egg into water. Repeat with 3 more eggs.

3. Cook, uncovered, 2-4 minutes or until whites are completely set and yolks begin to thicken but are not hard. Using a slotted spoon, lift eggs out of water. Repeat with remaining 4 eggs.

4. Top each muffin half with a slice of bacon, a poached egg and 2 Tbsp. sauce; sprinkle with paprika. Serve immediately.

1 SERVING: 345 cal., 26g fat (14g sat. fat), 331mg chol., 522mg sod., 15g carb. (1g sugars, 1g fiber), 13g pro.

EGGS BENEDICT WITH HOMEMADE HOLLANDAISE TIPS

What goes well with eggs Benedict? Most brunch foods pair wonderfully with this versatile dish! Serve it with a side of home fries and sauteed spinach, or even a light frisee salad to cut the richness of the sauce.

Is hollandaise sauce safe to eat? Yes, hollandaise sauce is safe to eat because the egg yolks are cooked over a double boiler until they reach 160°, which is the FDA's stated safe temperature.

Why do they call it eggs Benedict? Stories vary, but eggs a la Benedict (later shortened to eggs Benedict) were likely invented at New York's Delmonico's Restaurant or Waldorf Hotel in the late 1800s for a customer named Mrs. LeGrand Benedict.

LIGHT & FLUFFY WAFFLES

These melt-in-your-mouth waffles are so tender that you can skip butter and syrup—but why would you want to?
—James Schend, Pleasant Prairie, WI

PREP: 15 MIN. + STANDING • **COOK:** 5 MIN./BATCH • **MAKES:** 12 WAFFLES

- 2 large eggs
- 1½ cups all-purpose flour
- ½ cup cornstarch
- 1 tsp. baking powder
- ½ tsp. baking soda
- ½ tsp. salt
- ½ cup 2% milk
- 5 Tbsp. canola oil
- 2 tsp. vanilla extract
- 1 tsp. white vinegar
- 2 Tbsp. sugar
- ½ cup club soda, chilled
  Optional: Butter and maple syrup

1. Separate eggs. Place egg whites in a clean, dry bowl; let stand at room temperature 30 minutes.

2. In another bowl, whisk together next 5 ingredients. In a small bowl, whisk egg yolks, milk, oil, vanilla and vinegar until blended. Beat egg whites until soft peaks form. Gradually add sugar; continue beating until stiff peaks form.

3. Preheat waffle maker. Stir together flour mixture, egg yolk mixture and club soda just until combined. Fold egg whites into batter. Bake waffles according to manufacturer's directions until golden brown. Serve with butter and maple syrup if desired.

2 WAFFLES: 312 cal., 14g fat (2g sat. fat), 64mg chol., 421mg sod., 39g carb. (5g sugars, 1g fiber), 6g pro.

LIGHT & FLUFFY WAFFLES TIPS

Mix dry ingredients first, using a whisk, flour sifter or mesh strainer to distribute baking powder evenly throughout the mixture.

Replace some of the flour with cornstarch to guarantee a waffle that's crispy on the outside with a fluffy texture inside

Beating egg whites may seem like an extra step, but it's crucial to keep the waffles light and to give them some structure.

Using club soda instead of water in waffle or crepe batter makes a finished food that's nice and fluffy. Try it in puff pancake recipes too!

Gently fold the egg whites into the batter so you don't deflate them or overwork the batter. A few streaks of egg white left in the batter is just fine.

MAKE-AHEAD TECHNIQUES

To feed a crowd, keep waffles warm in a single layer on a baking sheet in a 200° oven.

For a quick and easy breakfast later, lay leftover waffles on a cookie sheet and place in the freezer. Then stack frozen waffles between sheets of waxed paper, place in a freezer bag and return to the freezer. Reheat in the toaster for a few minutes. Step aside, Eggo!

HOW TO JULIENNE PEPPERS

Step 1: Trim stem from pepper so it sits flat on its top.

Step 2: Cut 1 side off the pepper, being careful to leave the seeds and core intact.

Step 3: Rotate pepper and cut off another side. Continue turning and cutting until only the core remains; trim or discard core.

Step 4: Cut each pepper fillet into thin strips.

OPEN-FACED BREAKFAST BANH MI

I love banh mi sandwiches with delicious pickled veggies. I also love naan, so I combined the two for a fun breakfast!
—Lori McLain, Denton, TX

PREP: 25 MIN. + STANDING • **COOK:** 15 MIN. • **MAKES:** 4 SERVINGS

1 cup rice vinegar	½ lb. smoked sausage, thinly sliced
½ cup water	4 large eggs, room temperature
¼ cup sugar	4 naan flatbreads, warmed
½ tsp. salt	¼ cup zesty bell pepper relish
¼ tsp. pepper	½ cup thinly sliced cucumber
⅓ cup thinly sliced radishes	½ cup thinly sliced red onion
⅓ cup julienned carrot	Fresh cilantro leaves
⅓ cup julienned sweet red pepper	

1. In a large bowl, combine the first 5 ingredients; whisk until sugar is dissolved. Add radishes, carrot and red pepper; let stand until serving. Meanwhile, in a large nonstick skillet, cook and stir smoked sausage over medium-high heat until browned, 6-8 minutes. Remove and keep warm. Reduce heat to low. In the same pan, cook eggs until whites are set and yolks begin to thicken, turning once if desired. Keep warm.

2. Drain vegetable mixture. Spread naan with relish. Top with sausage, eggs, pickled vegetables, cucumber, red onion and cilantro.

1 OPEN-FACED SANDWICH: 459 cal., 24g fat (9g sat. fat), 229mg chol., 1370mg sod., 42g carb. (12g sugars, 2g fiber), 19g pro.

FLUFFY SCRAMBLED EGGS

When our son, Chris, wants something other than cold cereal in the morning, he whips up these eggs. Cheese and evaporated milk make them especially good. They're easy to make when you're camping too.
—Chris Pfleghaar, Elk River, MN

TAKES: 15 MIN. • **MAKES:** 3 SERVINGS

6 large eggs	⅛ tsp. pepper
¼ cup evaporated milk or half-and-half cream	1 Tbsp. canola oil
¼ tsp. salt	2 Tbsp. cheese dip

In a bowl, whisk eggs, milk, salt and pepper. In a large skillet, heat oil over medium heat. Pour in egg mixture; stir in cheese sauce. Cook and stir until eggs are thickened and no liquid egg remains.

½ CUP: 246 cal., 18g fat (6g sat. fat), 438mg chol., 523mg sod., 4g carb. (4g sugars, 0 fiber), 15g pro.

CUSTOMIZE YOUR SCRAMBLED EGGS

The recipe above is a starting point for the best scrambled eggs. Beyond salt and pepper, there are lots of other ingredients you can stir into your morning scramble.

- **Cheese:** One of the easiest (and tastiest) ways to amp up the flavor of scrambled eggs is to add some cheese. For perfectly gooey results, add shredded cheese during the last 30 seconds of cooking.

- **Herbs and spices:** Have fresh herbs on hand? Add them to your eggs! Basil, dill and chives all are great stirred into fluffy scrambled eggs. You can also raid your spice rack and add in dashes of garlic, cayenne or whatever you fancy.

- **Veggies:** Add sauteed onions, mushrooms, spinach and more to your scrambled eggs for extra color and flavor.

- **Ham, bacon or breakfast sausage:** You can turn your scrambled eggs into a heartier skillet meal by adding in chopped-up ham, breakfast sausage or whatever protein you please.

- **Hot sauce:** While many folks like to douse their eggs with hot sauce once they're on the plate, you can infuse your eggs with spice from the very start. Just add a few dashes of your go-to hot sauce right into the egg mix.

EGG COOKERY POINTERS

Here are some ways to make raveworthy scrambled eggs.

Get Back to Basics.
Instead of using milk and cheese sauce, whisk the 6 eggs with 6 Tbsp. of water. Some cooks swear by this winning ratio.

Consider the Carryover.
The trick to perfectly cooked, infinitely fluffy and toothsome eggs is to keep carryover cooking in mind. If not plating immediately, take the eggs off the heat once most, but not all, of the liquid egg has scrambled. Heat from the pan will cause the eggs to continue cooking, which can result in overcooked eggs.

Stir in Sour Cream.
Finishing a large pan of scrambled eggs with sour cream makes them so delicious and creamy—and the bit of tang helps them keep a pretty pale yellow color too. This is great for when you're keeping a large batch of eggs hot on a buffet.

SWEETS & BAKING

From old-time doughnuts to genius gelato, dig in here to discover sweet treats and baked goods that you will be proud to share. Our how-to photos and tips will be your guide. You've got this!

MUDSLIDE CHEESECAKE

I love to change up cheesecakes with different liqueur flavorings. This mudslide version with coffee and Irish cream is my husband's favorite.
—Sue Gronholz, Beaver Dam, WI

PREP: 30 MIN. • **BAKE:** 1 HOUR + CHILLING • **MAKES:** 16 SERVINGS

- 1 cup chocolate wafer crumbs
- 3 Tbsp. sugar
- 2 Tbsp. butter, melted

FILLING
- 1 cup semisweet chocolate chips
- 4 pkg. (8 oz. each) cream cheese, softened
- 1½ cups sugar
- 4 Tbsp. all-purpose flour
- 4 large eggs, room temperature, lightly beaten
- 2 tsp. vanilla extract
- 2 Tbsp. coffee liqueur
- ¾ cup Irish cream liqueur

GANACHE
- ½ cup semisweet chocolate chips
- ¼ cup heavy whipping cream

1. Preheat oven to 325°. Wrap a double thickness of heavy-duty foil (about 18 in. square) around a greased 9-in. springform pan. Mix cookie crumbs and sugar; stir in butter. Press onto bottom of prepared pan.

2. To prepare filling, microwave chocolate chips on high until melted, about 1 minute. Beat cream cheese and sugar until smooth. Add flour; mix well. Add eggs and vanilla; beat on low speed just until blended. Measure out 2 cups batter, and stir in coffee liqueur; add melted chocolate chips and stir until blended. Pour over crust. Add Irish cream liqueur to remaining batter; spoon over chocolate layer. Place springform pan in a larger baking pan; add 1 in. hot water to larger pan.

3. Bake until center is just set and top appears dull, 60-75 minutes. Remove springform pan from water bath. Cool cheesecake on a wire rack 10 minutes. Loosen side from pan with a knife; remove foil. Cool 1 hour longer. Refrigerate overnight, covering when completely cooled.

4. For ganache, microwave chocolate chips and whipping cream on high until chips melt; cool slightly. Remove rim from pan; spread ganache on chilled cheesecake.

1 PIECE: 485 cal., 31g fat (16g sat. fat), 118mg chol., 280mg sod., 44g carb. (37g sugars, 1g fiber), 6g pro.

PLATE LIKE A PRO
A hot knife is the secret to cutting nice tidy slices of cake and cheesecake. You'll need a sharp knife, some hot water and a towel. Dip the blade in water to heat, then wipe dry and cut. Repeat each time for pretty slices with a clean edge.

PERFECTLY BAKED EACH TIME

A reliable way to test cheesecake and baked custard for doneness is to gently thump the side of pan or ramekin. If the custard wobbles as one unit (instead of rippling like a stone tossed in a pool), it's ready.

JUDY'S CHOCOLATE CHIP BANANA BREAD

I received this recipe from my co-worker and dear friend Judy more than 30 years ago. When she gave it to me she said, "You will never need another banana bread recipe." She was right. But I did add lots of chocolate chips for the chocolate lovers in my family.
—Debra Keiser, St. Cloud, MN

PREP: 20 MIN. • **BAKE:** 1 HOUR + COOLING • **MAKES:** 1 LOAF (16 PIECES)

½ cup butter, softened
1¼ cups sugar
2 large egg, room temperature
1 cup mashed ripe bananas (about 2 medium)
¼ cup buttermilk
1 tsp. vanilla extract
2 cups all-purpose flour
1 tsp. baking powder
¾ tsp. baking soda
½ tsp. salt
¾ cup semisweet chocolate chips
¼ cup chopped walnuts, optional

1. Preheat oven to 350°. Line bottom of a greased 9x5-in. loaf pan with parchment; grease paper.

2. In a large bowl, beat butter and sugar until crumbly. Add eggs, 1 at a time, beating well after each addition. Beat in bananas, buttermilk and vanilla. In another bowl, mix flour, baking powder, baking soda and salt; stir into creamed mixture. Fold in chocolate chips and, if desired, walnuts.

3. Transfer to prepared pan. Bake until a toothpick inserted in center comes out clean, 60-65 minutes. Cool 10 minutes before removing from pan to a wire rack; remove paper.

1 PIECE: 229 cal., 9g fat (5g sat. fat), 42mg chol., 212mg sod., 36g carb. (22g sugars, 1g fiber), 3g pro.

HOW TO MAKE THE PERFECT BANANA BREAD

• Mash it! Use a potato masher to mash ripe bananas. Choose bananas that are yellow with lots of brown spots (the kind you'd normally think are too ripe to eat on their own).

• If desired, sprinkle batter with additional walnuts, chocolate chips or coarse sugar before baking.

DUTCH APPLE PIE

This pie is absolutely delicious and sure to bring in a bushel of compliments. Serve with ice cream for a perfect treat.

—Virginia Olson, West Des Moines, IA

PREP: 45 MIN. + CHILLING • **BAKE:** 1 HOUR • **MAKES:** 8 SERVINGS

1¼ cups all-purpose flour
½ tsp. salt
½ cup shortening
¼ cup cold water

FILLING
5 large tart apples, peeled and thinly sliced
⅔ cup sugar

5 tsp. all-purpose flour
1¼ tsp. ground cinnamon

TOPPING
⅔ cup all-purpose flour
⅓ cup sugar
⅓ cup packed brown sugar
¼ cup cold butter

1. In a large bowl, combine flour and salt; cut in shortening until crumbly. Gradually add water, tossing with a fork until dough forms a ball. Shape into a disk; wrap and refrigerate 1 hour or overnight.

2. Preheat oven to 450°. On a lightly floured surface, roll dough to a ⅛-in.-thick circle; transfer to a 9-in. pie plate. Trim crust to ½ in. beyond rim of plate; flute edge.

3. For filling, place apples in crust. Combine sugar, flour and cinnamon; sprinkle over apples.

4. For topping, in a small bowl, combine flour and sugars; cut in butter until crumbly. Sprinkle over filling. Bake 10 minutes. Reduce oven setting to 350°; bake 50-60 minutes or until topping is golden brown and filling is bubbly. Cool on a wire rack.

1 PIECE: 463 cal., 18g fat (7g sat. fat), 15mg chol., 197mg sod., 73g carb. (46g sugars, 3g fiber), 4g pro.

GREAT REASON TO GO DUTCH

With its golden streusel crumb topping, Dutch apple pie is ideal for beginning bakers. Even if your bottom pie crust is imperfect and patched together, you'll still have a gorgeous, perfect-looking finished pie! The crumb topping is ultra forgiving. Mix in a little cinnamon or oats for added interest.

DUTCH APPLE PIE TIPS

What kind of apples should I use for Dutch apple pie? Granny Smiths are the go-to apples for this pie because they're tart and firm and keep their shape while providing a perfect balance to the sweet ingredients. Pink Lady and Braeburn apples are other good choices for baking.

What should I do if the topping browns too quickly while baking? Cover the pie with foil to prevent the crumb topping from browning too quickly.

Can I use store-bought pie crust to make Dutch apple pie? You bet. That will make this pie come together in no time flat.

STRAWBERRY GELATO

You'll love this smooth and creamy gelato with bright strawberry flavor and just a hint of sea salt and honey.
—Shelly Bevington, Hermiston, OR

PREP: 10 MIN. + CHILLING • **PROCESS:** 25 MIN./BATCH + FREEZING • **MAKES:** 12 SERVINGS

2	**cups whole milk**
2	**Tbsp. light corn syrup**
1	**Tbsp. honey**
¾	**cup sugar**
½	**tsp. sea salt**
2½	**cups fresh strawberries (about 12 oz.), halved**
½	**cup heavy whipping cream**
1	**tsp. lemon juice**

1. Place first 6 ingredients in a blender; cover and blend. While blending, gradually add cream, blending just until combined. Remove to a bowl; stir in lemon juice. Refrigerate, covered, until cold, about 4 hours.

2. Fill cylinder of ice cream maker no more than two-thirds full; freeze according to manufacturer's directions. (Refrigerate any remaining mixture until ready to freeze.)

3. Transfer ice cream to freezer containers, allowing headspace for expansion. Freeze until firm, 3-4 hours.

½ CUP: 160 cal., 6g fat (4g sat. fat), 18mg chol., 124mg sod., 26g carb. (25g sugars, 1g fiber), 2g pro.

TEST KITCHEN TIPS

- Gelato means "ice cream" in Italian, but it has a few key differences. While both contain milk, cream and sugar, gelato traditionally contains a higher proportion of milk than ice cream does. It also doesn't contain eggs. These changes make gelato a denser, lower-in-fat dessert than ice cream.

- This recipe makes 4¾ cups of strawberry mixture before freezing and yields about 6 cups after freezing. If you have a 1-qt. ice cream maker, you will probably need to make the gelato in 2 batches. Be sure to follow your manufacturer's instruction manual.

- Corn syrup and honey contribute to the smoothness of this frozen treat by preventing the formation of ice crystals.

- Fresh raspberries or blackberries can be substituted for the strawberries. If your berries are tart, you may want to add a touch more sugar or honey.

GIANT CINNAMON ROLL

This must-try cinnamon roll is all about the pillowy texture, the sweet spices and the homemade caramel drizzle.
—Leah Rekau, Milwaukee, WI

PREP: 30 MIN. + RISING • **BAKE:** 30 MIN. • **MAKES:** 12 SERVINGS

1 pkg. (¼ oz.) active dry yeast
½ cup warm water (110° to 115°)
½ cup heavy whipping cream, warmed (110° to 115°)
½ cup sugar
½ tsp. sea salt
3 to 4 cups all-purpose flour
1 large egg, room temperature, beaten
3 Tbsp. butter, melted

FILLING
¼ cup butter, softened
¼ cup sugar
1 Tbsp. ground cinnamon

TOPPING
1 cup sugar
2 Tbsp. water
6 Tbsp. butter
½ cup heavy whipping cream
1 tsp. sea salt

1. Dissolve yeast in warm water and whipping cream until foamy. In another bowl, combine sugar and salt; add 3 cups flour, yeast mixture, egg and melted butter. Stir until moistened. Add enough remaining flour to form a soft dough.

2. Turn onto a lightly floured surface; knead until smooth and elastic, 3-4 minutes. Place in a greased bowl, turning once to grease top. Cover; let rise in a warm place until doubled, about 30 minutes.

3. Punch down dough. Turn onto a lightly floured surface; roll into a 15x12-in. rectangle. Spread softened butter over dough. Sprinkle with sugar and cinnamon. Using a pizza cutter, cut into 2-in.-wide strips. Roll up 1 strip and place in the center of a greased 9-in. deep-dish pie plate; wrap remaining strips around center to form 1 giant roll. Cover with greased foil; let rise until doubled, about 1 hour. Meanwhile, preheat oven to 350°.

4. Bake until golden brown, 30-40 minutes. If dough starts browning too quickly, cover lightly with foil. Cool on a wire rack.

5. To prepare topping, combine sugar and water in a small saucepan; cook over medium heat until it turns light amber. Add butter, stirring vigorously. Remove from heat; add cream while continuing to stir vigorously. Cool slightly. Pour ¾ cup sauce over warm roll; sprinkle with salt. Serve with remaining sauce.

1 PIECE: 416 cal., 21g fat (13g sat. fat), 76mg chol., 354mg sod., 55g carb. (30g sugars, 1g fiber), 5g pro.

TEST KITCHEN TIP
Reduce proofing (rising) times by giving your dough a toasty place to hang out. If your kitchen is cold, microwave a bit of water to create a sauna, then add the bowl of dough to the microwave and close the door. Happy yeast, happy roll!

CRUSHING CANDY CANES

To quickly (and neatly!) crush candy canes, place the candies in a heavy-duty resealable bag and crush them with a rolling pin.

PEPPERMINT LAVA CAKES

It never ceases to amaze to see warm chocolate pudding ooze out of the center of this tender chocolate cake. These cakes are always a showstopper! Serve lava cakes with whipped cream or ice cream.
—Carolyn Crotser, Colorado Springs, CO

TAKES: 30 MIN. • **MAKES:** 4 SERVINGS

- ⅔ cup semisweet chocolate chips
- ½ cup butter, cubed
- 1 cup confectioners' sugar
- 2 large eggs, room temperature
- 2 large egg yolks, room temperature
- 1 tsp. peppermint extract
- 6 Tbsp. all-purpose flour
- 2 Tbsp. crushed peppermint candies

1. Preheat oven to 425°. In a microwave-safe bowl, melt chocolate chips and butter for 30 seconds; stir until smooth. Whisk in confectioners' sugar, eggs, egg yolks and extract until blended. Fold in flour.

2. Transfer to 4 generously greased 4-oz. ramekins. Bake on a baking sheet until a thermometer reads 160° and edges of cakes are set, 14-16 minutes.

3. Remove from oven; let stand 5 minutes. Run a knife around sides of ramekins; invert onto dessert plates. Sprinkle with crushed candies. Serve immediately.

1 SERVING: 575 cal., 36g fat (21g sat. fat), 246mg chol., 227mg sod., 60g carb. (47g sugars, 2g fiber), 7g pro.

CITRUS LAVA CAKES

You may substitute ¾ tsp. orange extract and 1½ tsp. grated orange zest mixed with 1 Tbsp. coarse sugar for the peppermint extract and peppermint candies.

AIR-FRIED VARIATION
Preheat air fryer to 375°. Generously grease and flour four 4-oz. ramekins. Prepare batter; pour into ramekins. Do not overfill. Place ramekins on tray in air-fryer basket; cook until a thermometer reads 160° and edges of cakes are set, 10-12 minutes. Do not overcook.

Remove from basket; let stand 5 minutes. Run a knife around sides of ramekins several times to loosen cakes; invert onto dessert plates.

MERINGUE SNOWBALLS IN CUSTARD

My family has passed down this elegant dessert generation by generation. It started with my Russian great-grandmother, who traveled to America more than 100 years ago. I love continuing the tradition with her recipe.
—Tonya Burkhard, Palm Coast, Fl

PREP: 5 MIN. + STANDING • **COOK:** 20 MIN. + CHILLING • **MAKES:** 12 SERVINGS

4 **large egg whites**
4 **large egg yolks plus 2 large eggs**
1½ **cups sugar, divided**
1 **Tbsp. cornstarch**
6¼ **cups whole milk, divided**
2 **tsp. vanilla extract, divided**
½ **tsp. cream of tartar**
    Chopped glazed pecans, optional

1. Place egg whites in a large bowl; let stand at room temperature for 30 minutes. In a large heavy saucepan, whisk egg yolks, eggs, 1 cup sugar and cornstarch until blended; stir in 4 cups milk. Cook over medium-low heat 10-15 minutes or until mixture is just thick enough to coat a metal spoon and a thermometer reads at least 160°, stirring constantly. Do not allow to boil. Remove from heat immediately. Strain through a fine-mesh strainer into a large bowl.

2. Place bowl in an ice-water bath. Stir occasionally for 5 minutes. Stir in 1½ tsp. vanilla. Press plastic wrap onto surface of custard. Refrigerate until cold, about 1 hour.

3. For snowballs, add cream of tartar to egg whites; beat on medium speed until foamy. Gradually add remaining sugar, 1 Tbsp. at a time, beating on high after each addition until sugar is dissolved. Stir in remaining vanilla. Continue beating until stiff glossy peaks form.

4. In a large heavy skillet, bring remaining milk barely to a simmer over medium-low heat. Working in batches and using 2 soup spoons, drop meringue by ⅓ cupfuls into milk; poach meringues 4-6 minutes or until firm to the touch, turning once. Using a slotted spoon, remove meringues to paper towels to drain. Repeat with remaining meringue, making a total of 12 snowballs. (Discard remaining milk.) If desired, serve with pecans.

½ CUP SAUCE WITH 1 SNOWBALL: 216 cal., 6g fat (3g sat. fat), 105mg chol., 88mg sod., 32g carb. (31g sugars, 0 fiber), 7g pro.

HOW TO BEAT EGG WHITES TO STIFF PEAKS

- For maximum volume, use a very clean bowl and beaters.

- Let egg whites stand at room temperature 30 minutes.

- Lift beater out of the whites to test the peaks. Stiff peaks form a point rather than a soft or curving mound.

RASPBERRY
RUMBLE

CHOCOLATE
FUDGE

PEANUT BUTTER
M&M

ROCKY ROAD

CHOCOLATE FUDGE BROWNIES

My children always looked forward to these after-school snacks. They're so fudgy they don't need icing.
—Hazel Fritchie, Palestine, IL

PREP: 15 MIN. • **BAKE:** 35 MIN. + COOLING • **MAKES:** 16 SERVINGS

1 cup butter, cubed	1 tsp. vanilla extract
6 oz. unsweetened chocolate, chopped	½ tsp. salt
4 large eggs, room temperature	1 cup all-purpose flour
2 cups sugar	2 cups chopped walnuts
	Confectioners' sugar, optional

1. Preheat oven to 350°. In a small saucepan, melt butter and chocolate over low heat. Cool slightly.

2. In a large bowl, beat eggs, sugar, vanilla and salt until blended. Stir in chocolate mixture. Add flour, mixing well. Stir in walnuts.

3. Spread into a greased 9-in. square baking pan. Bake 35-40 minutes or until a toothpick inserted in center comes out with moist crumbs (do not overbake).

4. Cool completely in pan on a wire rack. If desired, dust with confectioners' sugar. Cut into bars.

1 BROWNIE: 410 cal., 28g fat (12g sat. fat), 77mg chol., 186mg sod., 36g carb. (26g sugars, 3g fiber), 6g pro.

DISH TOWEL PREVENTS SLIPPING
Need an extra hand in the kitchen? Take a cue from professional chefs and place a damp dish towel under your mixing bowl.

This keeps the bowl from sliding away (or worse) while you are mixing. It lets you have a hand free for adding other ingredients.

Place a damp towel under your cutting board for the same stability.

MAKE IT YOUR OWN WITH TOPPERS & MIX-INS

Customize your brownie with these delectable ideas.

• **Raspberry Rumble:** Mash ¼ cup fresh raspberries and stir into the batter. Add a few berries on top if you have them.

• **Peanut Butter M&M:** Add peanut butter M&M's to the batter, bake, then top with fudge frosting. Finish it off with a sprinkling of chopped peanut butter M&M's.

• **Rocky Road:** Pile on mini marshmallows and chopped pecans during the last 5 minutes of baking. Generously drizzle finished brownies with chocolate sauce.

FUNFETTI ICE CREAM CAKE

When we were young, Mom made birthday cakes with a small toy on top, chosen just for us. Now that I'm a parent, I go with sprinkles.
—Becky Herges, Fargo, ND

PREP: 50 MIN. + FREEZING • **MAKES:** 12 SERVINGS

4   cups birthday cake-flavored ice cream or flavor of your choice, softened if necessary
1   funfetti cake mix (regular size)

1   carton (8 oz.) frozen whipped topping, thawed
Sprinkles

1. Line a 9-in. round pan with plastic wrap. Spread ice cream into pan. Freeze 2 hours or until firm.

2. Prepare and bake cake mix according to package directions, using two 9-in. round baking pans. Cool in pans 10 minutes before removing to wire racks to cool completely.

3. Using a serrated knife, trim tops of cakes if domed. Place 1 cake layer on a serving plate. Invert ice cream onto cake layer; remove plastic wrap. Top with remaining cake layer. Spread whipped topping over top and side of cake. Decorate with sprinkles as desired. Freeze 2 hours longer or until firm.

1 PIECE: 374 cal., 19g fat (8g sat. fat), 66mg chol., 315mg sod., 45g carb. (27g sugars, 1g fiber), 5g pro.

ICE CREAM CAKE TIPS

What other flavor combinations can you use for this ice cream cake recipe? There are countless combinations you can try. How about coffee ice cream and German chocolate cake? Or consider strawberry ice cream with white or yellow cake. You could also skip the sprinkles or get creative with garnishes such as toasted nuts, flaked coconut, your favorite candies or freeze-dried berries.

Can you make your own frozen whipped topping for ice cream cake? You can make your own sweetened whipped cream to serve alongside any dessert, but not for frosting and freezing this ice cream cake. Frozen whipped topping is emulsified, so it freezes well and is easy to work with. It also has a bright white appearance.

Will an ice cream cake melt in the fridge? Yes! Ice cream cake will melt in the fridge, so be sure to keep leftovers in the freezer.

SEEING STARS

Mix red and blue sprinkles into white cake batter and vanilla ice cream. Top cake with star-shaped cookie cutters, then gently spoon nonpareils into each. Add sparklers to take it over the top!

UPSIDE-DOWN PEACH CAKE

Upside-down cake is a classic dessert that's really comforting. This one is very popular at my house.
—Terri Kirschner, Carlisle, IN

PREP: 15 MIN. • **BAKE:** 45 MIN. + COOLING • **MAKES:** 8 SERVINGS

¾ cup butter, softened, divided	1 tsp. vanilla extract
½ cup packed brown sugar	1¼ cups all-purpose flour
2 cups sliced peeled fresh peaches	1¼ tsp. baking powder
¾ cup sugar	¼ tsp. salt
1 large egg, room temperature	½ cup 2% milk

1. Melt ¼ cup butter; pour into an ungreased 9-in. round baking pan. Sprinkle with brown sugar. Arrange peach slices in a single layer over sugar.

2. In a large bowl, cream sugar and remaining butter until light and fluffy, 5-7 minutes. Beat in egg and vanilla. Combine the flour, baking powder and salt; add to creamed mixture alternately with milk, beating well after each addition. Spoon over peaches.

3. Bake at 350° until a toothpick inserted in the center comes out clean, 45-50 minutes. Cool for 10 minutes before inverting onto a serving plate. Serve warm.

1 PIECE: 384 cal., 19g fat (11g sat. fat), 71mg chol., 306mg sod., 52g carb. (36g sugars, 1g fiber), 4g pro.

PICKING PEACHES

At-peak, peaches will smell sweet and fragrant. They should be somewhat firm—not too hard or soft. If the fruit is green, it likely won't ripen well.

- **Freestone peaches:** The pit falls freely from (rather than clinging to) the fruit, making these popular for snacking on whole. Freestones come in white-fleshed and yellow-fleshed varieties. White peaches are more delicate tasting, making them great for eating fresh. Traditional yellow peaches are more intensely flavored, and they are better for baking, canning and other recipes.

- **Flat Peaches:** These squat-shaped peaches are sometimes labeled doughnut or Saturn peaches. They have white flesh and a small pit that's easily removed. These are sweet and juicy with a creamy texture.

- **Nectarines:** Yep—a nectarine really is a variety of peach! Only one small recessive gene variant separates nectarines from peaches, giving them a smooth skin that some people prefer.

UPSIDE-DOWN CAKE TIPS

How do you flip a cake upside-down? Flip it quickly and carefully, being sure to protect your body. Once the cake tests done, let it stand 10 minutes or as long as the recipe directs. (Larger cakes stand for longer than small ones.)

Place a serving plate upside-down over the cake. Wear oven mitts if you're able, but the most important thing when flipping the cake is to keep the serving plate firmly aligned over (to catch!) the cake. If you can't wear mitts, protect yourself with hot pads or kitchen towels. Flip the cake in 1 smooth, easy movement, placing it plate-side-down on the counter. Then gently wiggle and lift the baking pan away.

What if you wait too long? Just pop your cake back in the oven for a moment to help it warm up for a neat release.

How long will this cake last? Sweet upside-down cakes are best served warm, the day they're made. But you can cool, then cover and refrigerate the leftovers for 2-3 days. Warm a piece up in the microwave to reignite that caramelly magic!

HOT CHOCOLATE BOMBS

These indulgent, fun-filled spheres are all the rage! Make them ahead of time as a holiday gift or to have on hand when you have a hot chocolate craving.
—Rashanda Cobbins, Milwaukee, WI

PREP: 45 MIN. + CHILLING • **MAKES:** 6 CHOCOLATE BOMBS

22 oz. semisweet chocolate, such as Baker's Chocolate, finely chopped
½ cup baking cocoa
½ cup nonfat dry milk powder
¼ cup confectioners' sugar

6 Tbsp. vanilla marshmallow bits (not miniature marshmallows)
Optional: Sprinkles, colored sanding sugar and melted candy melts

1. Place chocolate in a microwave-safe bowl. Microwave, uncovered, on high for 1 minute; stir. Microwave, stirring every 30 seconds, until melted and smooth, 1-2 minutes longer. Chocolate should not exceed 90°.

2. Add 1 Tbsp. melted chocolate to a silicone sphere-shaped mold (2½-in. diameter). Brush melted chocolate evenly inside molds, all the way to edges, rewarming chocolate as needed. Refrigerate molds until chocolate is set, 3-5 minutes. Brush a thin second layer of chocolate in molds. Refrigerate until set, 8-10 minutes. Place remaining melted chocolate into a piping bag fitted with a small round decorating tip; set aside.

3. Remove chocolate hemispheres from molds. In a medium bowl, whisk together baking cocoa, milk powder and confectioners' sugar. Place 3 Tbsp. cocoa mixture into each of 6 of the chocolate hemispheres. Top with 1 Tbsp. marshmallow bits.

4. Pipe a small amount of melted chocolate on edges of the filled halves; carefully adhere empty halves to filled halves, pressing lightly to seal and using additional melted chocolate if necessary. Decorate if desired. Refrigerate until set. Store in a tightly sealed container.

1 CHOCOLATE BOMB: 619 cal., 34g fat (20g sat. fat), 1mg chol., 31mg sod., 36g carb. (29g sugars, 4g fiber), 10g pro.

MAKE IT YOUR OWN

- **Salted Caramel Hot Chocolate Bombs:** Fill spheres with hot cocoa mix, 1 Tbsp. caramel chips and a pinch of flaked sea salt. Drizzle outsides with melted dark chocolate and melted caramel chips; sprinkle with flaked sea salt.

- **Peppermint Hot Chocolate Bombs:** Fill spheres with hot cocoa mix, 1 Tbsp. white baking chips and 1 Tbsp. finely crushed peppermint candies. Drizzle outsides with melted white chocolate tinted pink and red; top with crushed peppermint candies.

SALTED CARAMEL

PEPPERMINT

THAT'S SWEET

To prepare hot chocolate, place hot chocolate bomb in a mug. Pour 1 cup hot milk over the top and stir to dissolve.

RESTORE
A RUSTED
CAST-IRON
SKILLET
Just hover your
camera here.

CHOCOLATE CHIP DUTCH BABY

I modified a traditional Dutch baby recipe given to me by a friend to come up with this version my family thinks is terrific. You'll be surprised at how easy it is to make.
—Mary Thompson, La Crosse, WI

TAKES: 30 MIN. • **MAKES:** 4 SERVINGS

¼ cup miniature semisweet chocolate chips
¼ cup packed brown sugar

DUTCH BABY

½ cup all-purpose flour
2 large eggs, room temperature
½ cup half-and-half cream
⅛ tsp. ground nutmeg
Dash ground cinnamon
3 Tbsp. butter
Optional: Maple syrup and additional butter

1. In a small bowl, combine chocolate chips and brown sugar; set aside. In another small bowl, beat the flour, eggs, cream, nutmeg and cinnamon until smooth.

2. Place butter in a 9-in. pie plate or an 8-in. cast-iron skillet. Heat in a 425° oven until melted, about 4 minutes. Pour batter into hot pie plate or skillet. Sprinkle with chocolate chip mixture. Bake until top edges are golden brown, 13-15 minutes. Serve immediately, with syrup and butter if desired.

1 PIECE: 313 cal., 17g fat (10g sat. fat), 144mg chol., 140mg sod., 33g carb. (21g sugars, 1g fiber), 6g pro.

FRUITY TAKES ON DUTCH BABY

- **Apple Dutch Baby:** Omit the chips, brown sugar, maple syrup and additional butter. Mix and bake Dutch baby as directed. Meanwhile, in a small saucepan, cook and stir 1 chopped peeled medium tart apple, ½ cup apple jelly and ⅛ tsp. ground cinnamon until jelly is melted. Top each serving with apple mixture.

- **Strawberry-Banana Dutch Baby:** Omit the chips, brown sugar, maple syrup and additional butter. Mix and bake Dutch baby as directed. Combine 2 sliced medium firm bananas and 1 cup sliced fresh strawberries. Top Dutch baby slices with fruit and, if desired, whipped cream; sprinkle each serving with 1 Tbsp. toasted flaked coconut.

APPLE PULL-APART BREAD

Drizzled with icing, each finger-licking piece of this bread has a yummy filling of apples and pecans. The recipe is well worth the bit of extra effort.
—Carolyn Gregory, Hendersonville, TN

PREP: 40 MIN. + RISING • **BAKE:** 35 MIN. + COOLING • **MAKES:** 16 SERVINGS

1 pkg. (¼ oz.) active dry yeast
1 cup warm 2% milk
½ cup butter, melted, divided
1 large egg, room temperature
⅔ cup plus 2 Tbsp. sugar, divided
1 tsp. salt
3 to 3½ cups all-purpose flour
1 medium tart apple, peeled and chopped
½ cup finely chopped pecans
½ tsp. ground cinnamon

ICING
1 cup confectioners' sugar
3 to 4½ tsp. hot water
½ tsp. vanilla extract

TRADITIONAL MIXING METHOD FOR YEAST BREADS

Step 1: Heat liquid to 110°-115°; check with a thermometer. Measure liquid, then pour into a large bowl. Add active dry yeast and stir until yeast is dissolved.

Step 2: Add sugar, salt, fat, eggs (if using) and about half the flour. Beat with an electric mixer or by hand until smooth.

Step 3: Stir in enough of the remaining flour by hand to form a dough of the consistency stated in the recipe.

1. In a large bowl, dissolve yeast in milk. Add 2 Tbsp. butter, egg, 2 Tbsp. sugar, salt and 3 cups flour; beat until smooth. Add enough remaining flour to form a stiff dough. Turn onto a floured surface; knead until smooth and elastic, 6-8 minutes. Place in a greased bowl, turning once to grease top. Cover and let rise in a warm place until doubled, about 1 hour.

2. Combine the apple, pecans, cinnamon and remaining sugar; set aside. Punch dough down; divide in half. Cut each half into 16 pieces. On a lightly floured surface, pat or roll out each piece into a 2½-in. circle. Place 1 tsp. apple mixture in center of circle; pinch edges together and seal, forming a ball. Dip in remaining butter.

3. In a greased 10-in. tube pan, place 16 balls, seam side down; sprinkle with ¼ cup apple mixture. Layer remaining balls; sprinkle with remaining apple mixture. Cover and let rise until nearly doubled, about 45 minutes.

4. Bake bread at 350° for 35-40 minutes or until golden brown. Cool for 10 minutes; remove from pan to a wire rack. Combine icing ingredients; drizzle over warm bread.

1 SERVING: 248 cal., 9g fat (4g sat. fat), 31mg chol., 218mg sod., 38g carb. (19g sugars, 1g fiber), 4g pro.

HOW TO ZEST A LEMON (3 WAYS)

- Our favorite way is with a rasp, a hand-held grater that makes ready-to-use, superfine zest.

- Using the finest side of a box grater is another technique. Be careful not to grate too far down through the peel, as the pale-colored pith tastes bitter.

- A citrus zester or channel knife makes narrow strips of zest, which you can use whole in drinks or finely minced in recipes.

SHORTBREAD LEMON BARS

I've put together two family cookbooks over the years, and this recipe ranks among my favorites. The special lemon bars have a yummy shortbread crust and refreshing flavor. I'm never afraid to make this dessert for guests because I know it will be a hit with everyone.
—Margaret Peterson, Forest City, IA

PREP: 25 MIN. • **BAKE:** 15 MIN. + CHILLING • **MAKES:** 3 DOZEN

1½ cups all-purpose flour	¼ cup all-purpose flour
½ cup confectioners' sugar	2 tsp. grated lemon zest
1 tsp. grated lemon zest	2 tsp. grated orange zest
1 tsp. grated orange zest	1 tsp. baking powder
¾ cup cold butter, cubed	

FILLING

TOPPING

4 large eggs

2 cups sour cream

2 cups sugar

⅓ cup sugar

⅓ cup lemon juice

½ tsp. vanilla extract

1. Preheat oven to 350°. In a food processor, combine the flour, confectioners' sugar, and lemon and orange zest. Add butter; cover and process until mixture forms a ball.

2. Pat into a greased 13x9-in. baking pan. Bake until set and the edges are lightly browned, 12-14 minutes.

3. In a large bowl, combine all the filling ingredients. Pour over hot crust. Bake until set and lightly browned, 14-16 minutes. In a small bowl, combine topping ingredients. Spread over filling.

4. Bake until topping is set, 7-9 minutes longer. Cool on a wire rack. Refrigerate overnight. Cut into bars just before serving. Store in the refrigerator.

1 BAR: 172 cal., 9g fat (5g sat. fat), 51mg chol., 70mg sod., 20g carb. (15g sugars, 0 fiber), 2g pro.

SHORTBREAD COOKIE TIPS

Cutting cold butter into dry ingredients results in tiny bits of flour-coated butter throughout the dough, creating a cookie crust that is both tender and crumbly at the same time. This recipe saves time with a food processor, but you could also cut in the butter with a pastry blender or 2 butter knives.

VANILLA CREAM FRUIT TART

It's well worth the effort to whip up this creamy tart bursting with juicy summer berries. A friend gave me the recipe, and it always receives rave reviews at gatherings.
—Susan Terzakis, Andover, MA

PREP: 25 MIN. • **BAKE:** 25 MIN. + CHILLING • **MAKES:** 12 SERVINGS

¾ cup butter, softened	½ cup pineapple juice
½ cup confectioners' sugar	¼ cup sugar
1½ cups all-purpose flour	1 Tbsp. cornstarch
1 pkg. (10 to 12 oz.) white baking chips, melted and cooled	½ tsp. lemon juice
¼ cup heavy whipping cream	4 cups assorted fresh fruit
1 pkg. (8 oz.) cream cheese, softened	

1. Preheat oven to 300°. Cream butter and confectioners' sugar until light and fluffy. Beat in flour (mixture will be crumbly). Pat onto a greased 12-in. pizza pan. Bake until lightly browned, 25-28 minutes. Cool.

2. Beat melted chips and cream until smooth. Beat in cream cheese until smooth. Spread over crust. Refrigerate 30 minutes. Meanwhile, in a small saucepan, combine pineapple juice, sugar, cornstarch and lemon juice. Bring to a boil over medium heat; cook and stir until thickened, about 2 minutes. Cool.

3. Arrange fruit over cream cheese layer; brush with pineapple mixture. Refrigerate 1 hour before serving.

1 PIECE: 433 cal., 28g fat (17g sat. fat), 60mg chol., 174mg sod., 43g carb. (28g sugars, 2g fiber), 5g pro.

FRUIT TART TIPS

What fruits can you use on a fruit tart? The beauty of this recipe is that you can use nearly any fruit. Berries, stone fruit and tropical fruits like mango all work well. The only fruits you should steer clear of are ones that brown when they are sliced, like apples, bananas and pears. Though they will taste fine, they won't look as appealing.

How do you keep fruit tarts from getting soggy? Most fruit tarts are best eaten on the day they are made to avoid sogginess. However, if you plan on keeping your fruit tart longer than a day, consider coating the crust with a thin layer of melted chocolate—it can be white, semisweet, milk or dark chocolate—prior to filling. Not only does it coat the crust and keep it from absorbing moisture, but it also adds an additional surprise element of flavor!

How long does a fruit tart last in the fridge? Fresh fruit tarts really last only 1-2 days in the fridge, loosely covered. It's best eaten sooner rather than later! If you want to prep this fruit tart ahead of time, make the filling and crust in advance and assemble on the day that you're serving it.

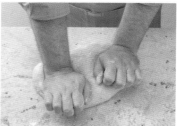

HAWAIIAN SWEET ROLLS

These sweet rolls are very similar to the kind found in bakeries—only better! Pineapple adds just the right amount of sweetness. My husband can't eat just one.
—Bernice Morris, Marshfield, MO

PREP: 35 MIN. + RISING • **BAKE:** 15 MIN. • **MAKES:** 2 DOZEN

1   pkg. (¼ oz.) active dry yeast
¼   cup warm water (110° to 115°)
1   Tbsp. plus ¼ cup sugar, divided
1   cup warm 2% milk (110° to 115°)
½   cup butter, melted, divided
2   large eggs, room temperature, lightly beaten
1   tsp. salt
5   to 5½ cups all-purpose flour

TOPPING
1½   tsp. cornstarch
1   can (8 oz.) crushed pineapple, undrained

GLAZE
1½   cups confectioners' sugar
1   tsp. vanilla extract
1   to 2 Tbsp. 2% milk

1. In a large bowl, dissolve yeast in warm water. Add 1 Tbsp. sugar; let stand 5 minutes. Add milk, ¼ cup butter, eggs, salt, remaining sugar and 1½ cups flour. Beat until smooth. Stir in enough remaining flour to form a soft dough.

2. Turn onto a floured surface; knead 6-8 minutes or until smooth and elastic. Place in a greased bowl, turning once to grease top. Cover and let rise in a warm place until doubled, about 45 minutes.

3. Punch dough down. Turn onto a floured surface; divide in half. Roll each into a 12x8-in. rectangle. Brush each with about 1 Tbsp. remaining butter. Roll up, jelly-roll style, starting with a long side. Pinch seam to seal.

4. Cut each into 12 slices. Place, cut side down, 2 in. apart on greased baking sheets. Brush with remaining butter. Cover and let rise in a warm place until doubled, about 30 minutes. Preheat oven to 425°.

5. Meanwhile, in a small saucepan, combine cornstarch and pineapple until blended. Bring to a boil over medium heat; cook and stir until thickened, 1-2 minutes. Remove from the heat.

6. Place a teaspoon of filling in the center of each roll. Bake until golden brown, 12-16 minutes. Remove from pans to wire racks.

7. For glaze, combine confectioners' sugar, vanilla and enough milk to achieve desired consistency. Drizzle over warm rolls.

1 SWEET ROLL: 188 cal., 5g fat (3g sat. fat), 29mg chol., 148mg sod., 32g carb. (12g sugars, 1g fiber), 4g pro.

COWBOY COOKIES

These cookies are very popular here in Wyoming. Mix up a batch for your crew and see why.
—Patsy Steenbock, Shoshoni, WY

PREP: 25 MIN. • **BAKE:** 15 MIN. • **MAKES:** 6 DOZEN

1 cup sweetened shredded coconut
¾ cup chopped pecans
1 cup butter, softened
1½ cups packed brown sugar
½ cup sugar
2 large eggs, room temperature
1½ tsp. vanilla extract
2 cups all-purpose flour
1 tsp. baking soda
½ tsp. salt
2 cups old-fashioned oats
2 cups (12 oz.) chocolate chips

1. Preheat oven to 350°. Place coconut and pecans on a 15x10x1-in. baking pan. Bake for 6-8 minutes or until toasted, stirring every 2 minutes. Set aside to cool.

2. In a large bowl, cream butter and sugars until light and fluffy, 5-7 minutes. Add eggs and vanilla; beat well. In another bowl, combine the flour, baking soda and salt. Add to creamed mixture; beat well. Stir in the oats, chocolate chips and toasted coconut and pecans.

3. Drop by rounded teaspoonfuls onto greased baking sheets. Bake at 350° about 12 minutes or until browned. Remove to wire racks to cool.

1 COOKIE: 105 cal., 6g fat (3g sat. fat), 12mg chol., 61mg sod., 14g carb. (9g sugars, 1g fiber), 1g pro.

MAKE 'EM TEXAS-SIZED

For hearty cowboy appetites, double the size of these cookies. Just make sure to increase the oven time, baking these until they're golden brown. Take care not to overbake, though. You want them to be crunchy on the outside and a bit chewy on the inside.

GET PORTIONS PERFECT WITH A COOKIE SCOOP

Bakers love sturdy cookie scoops with spring-release handles. They let you easily pop out dough in matching drops. There are many sizes available. A 1-Tbsp. size is useful for most cookie recipes.

BUCKEYE PIE

Everyone who eats this pie raves about it! You can cover the whole top with ganache, but leaving part of the filling bare is the traditional way to make it.
—Mary Northrup, Alpine, NY

PREP: 35 MIN. • **BAKE:** 10 MIN. + CHILLING • **MAKES:** 8 SERVINGS

CRUST
- 1¼ **cups chocolate wafer crumbs**
- ¼ **cup sugar**
- ¼ **cup butter, melted**

FILLING
- 1 **pkg. (8 oz.) cream cheese, softened**
- 1 **cup creamy peanut butter**
- ¾ **cup confectioners' sugar**
- 1 **tsp. vanilla extract**
- 1 **cup heavy whipping cream**

GANACHE
- ⅓ **cup semisweet chocolate chips**
- 2 **Tbsp. half-and-half cream**
- 2 **Tbsp. chopped salted peanuts**

1. Preheat oven to 350°. In a small bowl, combine crumbs, sugar and butter. Firmly press mixture onto bottom and up the side of a 9-in. pie plate. Bake until set, 10-12 minutes; cool completely.

2. In a large bowl, beat cream cheese until very smooth. Beat in peanut butter, sugar and vanilla. In a medium bowl, beat heavy cream until soft peaks form. Do not overbeat. Gently fold whipped cream into peanut butter mixture until fully incorporated. Pour into crust and spread evenly.

3. Place chocolate chips and half-and-half in a medium microwave-safe bowl. Microwave on high for 30 seconds; stir. Repeat until chocolate has melted and very smooth; do not overheat or chocolate may burn. Cool slightly.

4. Spread ganache over the peanut butter filling, leaving a 1-in. border of peanut butter filling uncovered around edge of pie. Sprinkle with chopped peanuts. Chill for several hours before serving.

1 PIECE: 559 cal., 41g fat (17g sat. fat), 56mg chol., 319mg sod., 43g carb. (32g sugars, 3g fiber), 10g pro.

SWEET ON BUCKEYES

Buckeye sweets combine peanut butter and chocolate flavors and are made to look like the inedible nuts of Ohio's state tree, the buckeye. The tree and nut get their name from the nut's resemblance to the eye of a white-tailed deer: shiny and dark on the outside, with a lighter center.

GARLIC FONTINA BREAD

With its golden brown color and soft texture, this bread is a must at any family meal. It's a modified version of a traditional white bread recipe my brother gave me. Try it as garlic bread toast, for grilled sandwiches or enjoy as is.
—Cindy Ryan, St. Johns, MI

PREP: 30 MIN. + RISING • **BAKE:** 30 MIN.
MAKES: 2 LOAVES (16 PIECES EACH)

2 pkg. (¼ oz. each) active dry yeast
2 cups warm water (110° to 115°)
3 Tbsp. sugar
2 Tbsp. shortening
1 Tbsp. garlic powder
2 tsp. salt
5 to 5½ cups all-purpose flour
1½ cups plus 2 Tbsp. shredded fontina cheese, divided
1½ tsp. canola oil

1. In a large bowl, dissolve yeast in warm water. Add sugar, shortening, garlic powder, salt and 3 cups flour. Beat until smooth. Stir in enough remaining flour to form a firm dough. Stir in 1½ cups cheese.

2. Turn onto a floured surface; knead until smooth and elastic, 6-8 minutes. Place in a greased bowl, turning once to grease the top. Cover and let rise in a warm place until doubled, about 1 hour. Preheat oven to 375°.

3. Punch dough down. Shape into 2 loaves. Place in 2 greased 9x5-in. loaf pans. Cover and let rise in a warm place until doubled, about 30 minutes. Brush with oil and sprinkle with remaining cheese.

4. Bake for 30-35 minutes or until golden brown. Cool on a wire rack.

1 PIECE: 119 cal., 4g fat (2g sat. fat), 10mg chol., 215mg sod., 17g carb. (2g sugars, 1g fiber), 4g pro.

STAGES OF WORKING YEAST BREAD

Kneading: Fold the top of the dough toward you. With your palms, push dough with a rolling motion away from you. Turn dough a quarter turn; repeat folding, kneading and turning until dough is smooth and elastic. Add a little flour to the counter as needed so dough doesn't stick.

Rising: Cover dough with a clean towel and let rise in a warm (80°-85°), draft-free area. To check if the dough has doubled in size, press 2 fingers about ½ in. into the dough. If the dents remain, the dough has doubled.

Punching down: Press your fist quickly but gently into the center of the dough, then form it into a ball and knead 2-3 times. After punching down, let dough rise a second time.

THICK STRAWBERRY SHAKES

Cool off with a thick and rich treat that will remind you of a malt shoppe!
—Kathryn Conrad, Milwaukee, WI

TAKES: 5 MIN. • **MAKES:** 2 SERVINGS

⅓ cup 2% milk
1½ cups vanilla ice cream
½ cup frozen unsweetened
   strawberries
1 Tbsp. strawberry preserves

In a blender, combine all ingredients; cover and process until smooth. Pour into chilled glasses; serve immediately.

1 CUP: 257 cal., 12g fat (7g sat. fat), 47mg chol., 100mg sod., 35g carb. (28g sugars, 1g fiber), 5g pro.

MILKSHAKE TIPS

- Put liquid into the blender first: This helps get the action started! Then add ice cream and flavorings and blend away.

- Use whole milk—or milk plus a little half-and-half cream— to get a really nice, rich texture. Do not use heavy cream— it will blend into little bits of butter.

- Individual tastes vary. Use less milk for a thick shake, and more for a thinner, more sippable shake.

- Begin with softened ice cream. If the ice cream is too hard, you may end up adding more liquid to get the milkshake to blend properly—and then when you're serving, the shake may be thinner than you'd like.

PUMPKIN SPICE SHEET CAKE WITH CREAM CHEESE FROSTING

The cream cheese frosting wonderfully complements this spice cake.
—Sandy McKenzie, Braham, MN

PREP: 20 MIN. • **BAKE:** 20 MIN. + COOLING • **MAKES:** 24 SERVINGS

1 **can (15 oz.) pumpkin**	2 **tsp. ground cinnamon**
1½ **cups sugar**	¼ **tsp. ground cloves**
4 **large eggs, room**	
temperature	FROSTING
1 **cup canola oil**	½ **cup butter, softened**
2 **cups all-purpose flour**	6 **oz. cream cheese, softened**
2 **tsp. baking powder**	2 **tsp. vanilla extract**
1 **tsp. baking soda**	4½ **cups confectioners' sugar**
¼ **tsp. salt**	24 **candy pumpkins, optional**

1. Preheat oven to 350°. Grease a 15x10x1-in. pan.

2. Beat together first 4 ingredients. In another bowl, whisk together flour, baking powder, baking soda, salt and spices; gradually beat into pumpkin mixture.

3. Transfer to prepared pan. Bake until a toothpick inserted in center comes out clean, 20-25 minutes. Cool completely in pan on a wire rack.

4. For frosting, beat butter, cream cheese and vanilla until smooth. Gradually beat in confectioners' sugar. Spread over cake. If desired, top with candy pumpkins. Refrigerate leftovers.

1 PIECE: 346 cal., 17g fat (5g sat. fat), 48mg chol., 184mg sod., 48g carb. (37g sugars, 1g fiber), 3g pro.

BASIC CAKE-MAKING TIPS

- Arrange oven racks so the cake will bake in the center of the oven.

- Bring all fat and dairy, including butter and eggs, to room temperature before you mix them for batter.

- Mix dry ingredients together with a whisk or sift them together to evenly distribute the leavener throughout the flour.

- Scrape the batter down the side of the bowl occasionally (after first turning off the mixer!).

- Fill pans halfway to three-quarters full. Thinner batters rise higher than thicker ones and should only fill the pan halfway.

- Pour thinner batters into pans, then tap pans on the counter to remove air bubbles. Spoon firmer batters into pans and spread gently with a spatula to even them out.

- If using more than 1 pan, there should be at least 1 inch of space between each pan and the sides of the oven to allow good heat circulation.

WATERMELON FRUIT PIZZA

Fruit pizza is an easy and refreshing way to end a summer meal. Top it with any fruit you may have on hand and add other toppings like fresh mint, toasted shredded coconut or chopped nuts.
—*Taste of Home* Test Kitchen

TAKES: 10 MIN. • **MAKES:** 8 SERVINGS

4 oz. cream cheese, softened
4 oz. frozen whipped topping, thawed
½ tsp. vanilla extract
3 Tbsp. confectioners' sugar

1 slice of whole seedless watermelon, about 1 in. thick
Assorted fresh fruit
Fresh mint leaves, optional

1. In a small bowl, beat cream cheese until smooth. Gently fold in the whipped topping, then the vanilla and confectioners' sugar until combined.

2. To serve, spread watermelon slice with frosting. Slice into 8 wedges and top with your fruit of choice. If desired, garnish with fresh mint.

1 PIECE: 140 cal., 7g fat (5g sat. fat), 14mg chol., 45mg sod., 17g carb. (16g sugars, 0 fiber), 1g pro. **DIABETIC EXCHANGES:** 1½ fat, 1 fruit.

PENNSYLVANIA DUTCH POTATO DOUGHNUTS

My relatives have been making these tasty doughnuts for years. The potatoes keep them moist, and the glaze provides just the right amount of sweetness.
—Marlene Reichart, Leesport, PA

PREP: 20 MIN. + CHILLING • **COOK:** 50 MIN. • **MAKES:** ABOUT 4 DOZEN

2½ cups mashed potatoes or riced potatoes (without added milk, butter or seasonings)
1 cup whole milk
3 large eggs, room temperature, lightly beaten
2 Tbsp. butter, melted
2 cups sugar
2 Tbsp. baking powder
5 to 6 cups all-purpose flour
Oil for deep-fat frying

GLAZE
2 cups confectioners' sugar
5 Tbsp. half-and-half cream
½ tsp. vanilla extract
Optional: Food coloring and sprinkles

1. In a large bowl, combine the potatoes, milk, eggs and butter. Combine the sugar, baking powder and 2 cups flour; stir into potato mixture. Add enough remaining flour to form a soft dough. Refrigerate, covered, 1 hour.

2. Divide dough in half. Turn each half onto a lightly floured surface; roll to ½-in. thickness. Cut with a 2¾-in. doughnut cutter.

3. In an electric skillet or deep-fat fryer, heat oil to 375°. Fry doughnuts, a few at a time, until golden brown on both sides. Drain on paper towels.

4. In a small bowl, mix glaze ingredients until smooth. Color glaze if desired. Dip doughnuts in glaze and sprinkles as desired.

1 DOUGHNUT: 163 cal., 6g fat (1g sat. fat), 14mg chol., 74mg sod., 25g carb. (14g sugars, 1g fiber), 2g pro.

MAKE IT YOUR OWN WITH FLAVORED GLAZES

- **Chocolate Glaze:** Bring ½ cup heavy whipping cream and 2 Tbsp. light corn syrup just to a boil; pour over 6 oz. chopped semisweet chocolate. Stir with a whisk until smooth. Stir in 2 tsp. vanilla extract.

- **Maple Glaze:** Whisk 2 cups confectioners' sugar, 3 Tbsp. 2% milk, 2 Tbsp. maple syrup and ½ tsp. maple flavoring until smooth.

HOW TO DECORATE DOUGHNUTS

To make decorating easy, use small bowls for different icing colors and sprinkles.

Dip doughnuts into glaze, then place on a wire rack and let stand until set. Or dip the just-glazed doughnuts into sprinkles.

COOKING GLOSSARY

AL DENTE An Italian term meaning "to the tooth." Used to describe pasta that is cooked but still firm.

BASTE To moisten food with melted butter, pan drippings, marinade or other liquid to add flavor and juiciness.

BEAT To mix rapidly with a spoon, fork, wire whisk or electric mixer.

BLEND To combine ingredients until just mixed.

BOIL To heat liquids until bubbles that cannot be stirred down are formed. In the case of water, the temperature will reach 212°.

BONE To remove all bones from meat, poultry or fish.

BROIL To cook food 4-6 in. from a direct, radiant heat source.

CREAM To blend ingredients to a smooth consistency by beating; frequently done with butter and sugar for baking.

CUT IN To break down and distribute cold butter, margarine or shortening into a flour mixture with a pastry blender or 2 knives.

DASH A measurement less than ⅛ tsp. that is used for herbs, spices and hot pepper sauce. This is not a precise measurement.

DREDGE To coat foods with flour or other dry ingredients. Most often done with pot roasts and stew meat before browning.

FLUTE To make a "V" shape or scalloped edge on pie crust with your thumb and fingers.

FOLD To blend dissimilar ingredients by careful and gentle turning with a spatula. Used most commonly to incorporate whipped cream, beaten egg whites, fruit, candy or nuts into a thick, heavy batter.

JULIENNE To cut foods into long, thin strips much like matchsticks. Used often for salads and stir-fries.

KNEAD To work dough by using a pressing and folding action to make it smooth and elastic.

MARINATE To tenderize and/or flavor foods, usually vegetables or raw meat, by placing them in a mixture of oil, vinegar, wine, lime or lemon juice, herbs and spices.

MINCE To cut into very fine pieces. Often used for garlic, hot peppers and fresh herbs.

PARBOIL To boil foods, usually vegetables, until partially cooked. Most often used when vegetables are to be finished using another cooking method or chilled for marinated salads or dips.

PINCH A measurement less than ⅛ tsp. that is easily held between the thumb and index finger. This is not a precise measurement.

PULSE To process foods in a food processor or blender with short bursts of power.

PUREE To mash solid foods into a smooth mixture with a food processor, mill, blender or sieve.

SAUTE To fry quickly in a small amount of fat, stirring almost constantly. Most often done with onions, mushrooms and other chopped vegetables.

SCORE To cut slits partway through the outer surface of foods. Often required for ham or flank steak.

SIMMER To cook liquids, or a combination of ingredients with liquid, at just under the boiling point (180-200°). The surface of the liquid will have some movement and there may be small bubbles around the sides of the pan.

STEAM To cook foods covered on a rack or in a steamer basket over a small amount of boiling water. Most often used for vegetables.

STIR-FRY To cook meats, grains and/or vegetables with a constant stirring motion, in a small amount of oil, or in a wok or skillet over high heat.

EQUIVALENT MEASURES

3 teaspoons	= 1 tablespoon	16 tablespoons	= 1 cup
4 tablespoons	= ¼ cup	2 cups	= 1 pint
5⅓ tablespoons	= ⅓ cup	4 cups	= 1 quart
8 tablespoons	= ½ cup	4 quarts	= 1 gallon

FOOD EQUIVALENTS

Macaroni	1 cup (3½ ounces) uncooked	= 2½ cups cooked
Noodles, medium	3 cups (4 ounces) uncooked	= 4 cups cooked
Popcorn	⅓–½ cup unpopped	= 8 cups popped
Rice, long grain	1 cup uncooked	= 3 cups cooked
Rice, quick-cooking	1 cup uncooked	= 2 cups cooked
Spaghetti	8 ounces uncooked	= 4 cups cooked
Bread	1 slice	= ¾ cup soft crumbs, ¼ cup fine dry crumbs
Graham crackers	7 squares	= ½ cup finely crushed
Buttery round crackers	12 crackers	= ½ cup finely crushed
Saltine crackers	14 crackers	= ½ cup finely crushed
Bananas	1 medium	= ⅓ cup mashed
Lemons	1 medium	= 3 tablespoons juice, 2 teaspoons grated zest
Limes	1 medium	= 2 tablespoons juice, 1½ teaspoons grated zest
Oranges	1 medium	= ¼–⅓ cup juice, 4 teaspoons grated zest
Cabbage	1 head	= 5 cups shredded
Carrots	1 pound	= 3 cups shredded
Celery	1 rib	= ½ cup chopped
Corn	1 ear fresh	= ⅔ cup kernels
Almonds	1 pound	= 3 cups chopped
Ground nuts	3¾ ounces	= 1 cup
Green pepper	1 large	= 1 cup chopped
Mushrooms	½ pound	= 3 cups sliced
Onions	1 medium	= ½ cup chopped
Potatoes	3 medium	= 2 cups cubed
Pecan halves	1 pound	= 4½ cups chopped
Walnuts	1 pound	= 3¾ cups chopped

RECIPE INDEX